Let thy soul

delight in thy

husband.

D&C 25:14

What Husbands Expect of Wives

Brent A. Barlow

Deseret Book Company
Salt Lake City, Utah

First printing in paperbound edition, April 1989

Library of Congress Catalog Card Number 83-070707

ISBN 0-87747-971-2 (hardbound ed.)
ISBN 0-87579-197-2 (paperbound ed.)

Printed in the United States of America

10 9 8 7 6 5 4 3

CONTENTS

PREFACE

President Spencer W. Kimball once observed, "While marriage is difficult, and discordant and frustrated marriages are common, yet real, lasting happiness is possible, and marriage can be more an exultant ecstasy than the human mind can conceive. *This is within the reach of every couple, every person.*"[1] (Italics added.)

This statement of President Kimball offers perspective and should give married couples both hope and confidence. I hope that what is contained in the pages that follow will contribute in some small way to help husbands and wives attain the fulfillment and even ecstasy that President Kimball spoke of.

A few months ago I had just finished a seminar on marriage for Brigham Young University Conferences and Workshops when one of the husbands who had attended approached me. "When are you going to write the blue book?" he asked. "Blue book?" I replied. "Yes, the blue book," he answered. I was puzzled for a moment and didn't know what he meant. Then he smiled and said "You wrote the pink book, *What Wives Expect of Husbands,* for men to read. Now why don't you write the blue book, *What Husbands Expect of Wives* for women to read?"

After *What Wives Expect of Husbands* was published in April 1982, I was constantly asked that same question or ones like it.

Now, for those who are interested, I am happy to have completed the blue book, *What Husbands Expect of Wives.* And I trust it will be helpful, not as a list of things wives are expected to do, but as a guide to improve couples' relationships.

In many ways, *What Husbands Expect of Wives* has been more difficult to write than the previous book. I have learned that many husbands are a little more hesitant to share their thoughts, feelings, and expectations than are wives. While most husbands are willing to fill out a checklist of expectations, relatively few are willing to write to any great extent their thoughts and concerns. This, in and of itself, was a significant finding. (And, by the way, it is why relatively few quotations from husbands will be found in this book.)

I was interested that husbands ranked communication number six in importance in marriage while wives far and away ranked it number one! Wives appear to have a higher need to discuss things with husbands than do husbands with wives. This finding simply verifies what Dr. Joyce Brothers recently noted in her bestselling book *What Every Woman Should Know About Men.* She wrote, "Men talk about themselves less." I agree.

Another difficulty with this book is what I call overkill. In many ways contemporary husbands and wives are overstimulated with the vast number of books, magazine and newspaper articles, television and radio talk shows, and the numerous admonitions from a variety of people on how to be better husbands, wives, and parents. Some even resent the constant bombardment from so many sources.

In planning and writing this book, I have often wondered if it would be just another source adding to the confusion or if it would actually be helpful. It seems that most women (particularly LDS women) do not need another book on how to be wonderful. I appreciate the humor and candor of Afton Day, who wrote the recent book *How to Be a Perfect Wife, and Other Myths.* Just for perspective, perhaps wives should read her book before proceeding with this one.

So why am I writing? There are several reasons.

First among them is the wide acceptance *What Wives Expect of Husbands* had with a number of people. Comments from many readers of that book have given me the encouragement to write this one.

Second, the many contacts I have had the past few years with husbands in classes, seminars, marriage counseling, and a *Deseret News* survey have convinced me that the chapters included here do cover some of the common expectations of most husbands. While husbands have been hesitant to write a great deal, more than three hundred have completed "Understanding Your Expectations" (appendix A) and indicated from a pool of twenty items that the ones included in this book are significant to them. (See appendix B.)

A third stimulus for writing has been my contact with many readers of my column on marriage in the *Deseret News.* During the past four years many readers have taken the time to write and share some of their thoughts and concerns about marriage. While I enjoy the academic life and its environment, I don't think anything gives me more incentive to write than reading some of the letters I receive. I do want to assist wherever possible and also desire to honor the trust and confidence demonstrated when readers share their concerns and questions about marriage.

Fourth, I feel those in the field of marriage and family, or wherever they may be, have an obligation and even responsibility to share their knowledge, skills, and insights. And writing a book like this one is one way this may be accomplished.

Finally, one statement by Elder Hugh B. Brown has given me considerable thought during the past few months about specific reasons why husbands and wives should become aware of each other's expectations and make genuine efforts to make these expectations realities. In his book *You and Your Marriage,* Elder Brown observed, "This program of enjoying things together, which begins in courtship, should not lapse, but continue through the early, middle, and later married years. The couple should not wait until the days of their active parenthood are past before undertaking their joint project of enriching life. If they have not learned along the way to be delightful, lively, interesting, and inquisitive, then when their active parenthood days are past, there is danger of their seeking the chimney corner, where, as querulous old people, they may huddle and commiserate."[2]

If this book gives just a few insights to husbands and particularly wives on how to be "delightful, lively, interesting, and inquisitive" in marriage, then I think the book is justified. But the reader will have to be the ultimate judge.

ACKNOWLEDGMENTS

I would like to thank the three hundred husbands who filled out the questionnaire "Understanding Your Expectations" (appendix A). These husbands responded to my request in my *Deseret News* column or were enrolled in my marriage seminar classes at Brigham Young University.

Thanks also to Don Woodward, editor of the "Today" section of the *Deseret News,* and to Carma Wadley and others on the *Deseret News* staff who have made possible my weekly column.

I also thank the Department of Family Sciences at Brigham Young University for providing secretarial help to type the original draft. The secretaries also provided valuable insights during the process. Thanks also to the Faculty Support Center of the College of Family, Home, and Social Sciences at BYU for providing help in proofreading the final manuscript.

Several people at Deseret Book were also helpful, not only for their encouragement for this book, but also for their professional expertise. Few people appreciate, I believe, the behind-the-scenes efforts of so many who prepare a book for publication. Among those at Deseret Book who greatly assisted were Lowell Durham, president; Eleanor Knowles, editor and publishing manager; Jack Lyon, associate editor, who edited this book; Ralph

Reynolds, design director; Carole Cole and Richard Tice, assistant editors; Jim McLaughlin, production manager; and Susan Conard, typesetter.

I also appreciate our six children, who held their comments to a minimum during the summer of 1982 while Dad spent a great deal of time writing "some book for women to read."

And finally, to my adorable wife, Susan, I say, "No, Susan, this book is not a personal fantasy or figment of my imagination, nor was it taken from my personal journal entries as you have suspected all along. I love you and appreciate your sensitivity to what this husband expected of his wife while trying to write this book."

1

LOVE

It should come as no great surprise to wives that husbands want to be loved, more so than anything else. It is a natural, basic need of all human beings. Many of the three hundred husbands who responded to my questionnaire in the *Deseret News* and during marriage seminars ranked love as the most important thing they expected from their wives.

In his book *The Art of Loving,* Dr. Erich Fromm has noted, "Love is the only satisfactory answer to the problem of human existence. Yet most of us are unable to develop our capacities for love on the only level that really counts—a love that is compounded of maturity, self-knowledge and courage. Learning to love, like other arts, demands practice and concentration. Even more than any other art it demands genuine insights and understanding."[1]

Periodically, it is good for husbands and wives to explore how they love each other and the way they express their love. Literally hundreds of books and articles have been written on love, so we will not resolve the whole issue of love in just one short chapter. But Dr. Fromm mentions that love "demands genuine insights and understanding," which I will attempt to give in the pages that follow.

Myths About Love and Marriage

Many couples become confused about marriage because they do not know if they are "really" in love or able to stay in love with the person they marry. Much of the time they judge what they are experiencing against what they think marriage should be like. It is just possible, however, that we believe some myths about love that can lead to marital turmoil.

At the beginning of our own marriage, Susan and I spent three weeks of wedded bliss before we had our first major disagreement. We were disappointed afterward because we both had somehow acquired the notion that there is little or no conflict in a good marriage. This idea, however, we later discovered to be one of the several myths we would encounter in marriage.

In their book *The Mirages of Marriage,* William J. Lederer and Dr. Don J. Jackson write, "We believe that if men and women were acquainted with the realities of marriage before they entered it, the divorce rate in the United States would diminish markedly."[2]

The authors then describe what they believe to be some of the major myths about marriage. See if you agree:

1. All people marry because they love each other.
2. Most married people romantically love each other.
3. A great deal of romantic love is necessary for a satisfactory marriage.
4. There are inherent behavioral and attitudinal differences between males and females, and these differences cause most marital troubles (for example, women are emotional and men are logical).
5. A potentially difficult marriage will automatically be improved by having children.
6. Loneliness will be cured by marriage.
7. If you have conflict in your marriage, you have a poor marriage.

In his article "Marriage of the Future," Dr. David H. Olson from the University of Minnesota has also written about marriage myths. He observes that "one of the reasons that the marriage institution does not live up to its expectations is because of the many myths and unrealistic expectations that individuals bring to marriage."[3] Dr. Olson lists what he thinks are some marriage myths:

1. If a sexual relationship is not good, it will spontaneously improve with time.
2. Marriage will always change or reform a person.
3. Marriage is easy; the difficulty is finding the right person.
4. Whom you marry is more important than when you marry.
5. Your marriage partner will be able to satisfy all your needs.
6. The more time spent and activities shared together, the better the marriage relationship.
7. Patterns of behavior and interaction that develop are easy to change.
8. A quarrel or disagreement can only be detrimental to a marriage.
9. It is always best not to express negative feelings about one's spouse.
10. If a married couple loves each other they will automatically know what each other is feeling or wanting.
11. A good sexual relationship in marriage will be automatic and easy to develop.
12. If there is a good sexual relationship in marriage, other problems will take care of themselves.
13. Sexual adjustment in marriage will result more from proper techniques than from proper attitudes.

You may or may not agree that all of the above are myths about marriage. There may be exceptions to each. It is evident, however, that many people are unhappy in their marriages and therefore many question their love because they have unrealistic expectations. Susan and I like this quotation of Robert Lewis Stevenson: "Marriage is one long conversation, chequered by disputes."

If You Love 'em, Tell 'em

Not long ago, The Church of Jesus Christ of Latter-day

Saints conducted three consecutive meetings on the theme "If You Love 'em, Tell 'em." One was held on Temple Square and the other two at Brighton High school in south Salt Lake City. I was invited to participate. At their meetings, the Church showed the best of their television Home Front series, which centered on the importance of telling family members you love them.

Some wives and husbands don't often say "I love you" to each other because they feel they bungle the job when they try. I once explained to a group that there are magic words in marriage we ought to say more often. These words are "Please forgive me," "I love you," and "I'm sorry." One wife called me up the next night and said the magic words didn't work.

"Exactly what did you say?" I asked. She said she walked up to her husband, took a deep breath, and blurted out, "I'm sorry I love you; please forgive me." I told her she had the content but her timing was off.

How are you and your marriage partner doing in the verbal expression of love? Do you express it often? Do you express it enough? Talk it over, and you may be surprised with what you find out.

I sincerely believe the vast majority of husbands and wives genuinely love each other. And I also believe "if you love 'em, tell 'em." Most marriage partners do not require a great deal of love to be satisfied in marriage. Rather than quantity, they just need a constant supply.

Love and the First Year of Marriage

Most engaged couples frequently tell each other of their love, and this trend usually continues into the first year of marriage. And what happens during that first year is of major concern to marriage educators and counselors. Which is the most critical year of marriage? Most husbands and wives would say, "The one we are in!" But there is increasing evidence that the first year of marriage is especially important.

Alexander Pope wrote, "As the twig is bent, the tree is inclined." And his statement is apparently true of marriage.

William George Jordan observed:

> In the days of courtship two may feel that they thoroughly understand each other, and that no matter how many marriages may fail *their* happiness together is absolutely assured. Yet courtship is only the kindergarten class of matrimony. Courtship is the preliminary canter, not the real race. It is the matrimonial shopping; marriage is the acceptance of the unreturnable delivered goods. Courtship is the joyous, sunshine launching of the craft of hope; marriage is the long cruise across uncharted seas. The two now pass under the test of new conditions; they face new problems and enter a life of finer attunement, of constant call on patience, tolerance, forbearance, concession, kindness, sympathy and wise understanding.[4]

It is significant that approximately 40 percent of all marriages in any one year that end in separation or divorce may do so by the end of the first five years. The causes of these broken marriages are often the unwise choice of marriage partners and the inability of the couple to meet life's problems during the first year of marriage.

It is interesting that the first year of marriage was so important to the ancient Hebrew family that young couples were given one year free from civic and other major responsibilities to adjust to each other and develop their love. In Deuteronomy 24:5 we read, "When a man hath taken a new wife, he shall not go out to war, neither shall he be charged with any business: but he shall be free at home one year, and shall cheer up his wife which he hath taken."

I recently read an article by Edward Bader and Carole Sinclair, "The Critical First Year of Marriage." They claim it is probably impossible to overestimate the importance of the first year of marriage.

So many key decisions and adjustments need to be worked out. For instance, will there be a dominant and a submissive role? Or will a balance of power be established? How will the money be managed? What frequency or pattern of lovemaking will be established? How will quarrels be resolved? Whatever patterns are established at the beginning of marriage will likely continue for many years, and the way these patterns develop can greatly influence the future of the marriage.[5]

If there is an appropriate time that professional, religious, civic, and other interested parties can extend help to married couples, the first year of marriage appears to be that time. I was impressed to learn that a church in Kansas City, Missouri, has recently started a successful education program for newlyweds, similar to the LDS Church's Family Relations class.

Most married couples can remember their first year of marriage. A few would prefer not to. But we learn how to have a good marriage over a period of time. Newlyweds ought not to become unduly discouraged during the first few months of their marriage. Just remember: Crisis + Time = Humor.

Remembering the Positive Things

Even though some difficult moments and times of adjustment occur during the first few years of marriages, there are some very pleasant times as well. We need to be careful to focus on the strengths of our marriages, not our weaknesses.

In my marriage classes and seminars we do an interesting exercise called "Marriage Strengths and Memories." The purpose of this exercise is to help couples recall together in writing some of the pleasant aspects of their marriages. Even when I am counseling couples who are on the verge of divorce, I can usually get them to realize they have had good times as well as bad. If we focus only on the difficult times, the marriage is viewed from a distorted perspective.

You and your spouse could complete the following sentences in writing and then share your responses with each other.

Memories

1. The first time I saw you was ———.
2. I wanted to be with you because ———.
3. I was impressed with you because ———.
4. I decided I wanted to marry you because ———.

5. During our engagement, the most difficult situations we overcame were ———.

6. My most pleasant memories of our wedding day are ———.

7. The most difficult experiences we have encountered and survived thus far in our marriage are ———.

8. At the birth of our first child I felt ———.

9. The highlights of our marriage thus far have been ———.

10. Other pleasant memories I have of you and our marriage are ———.

11. The things I like best about you are ———.

12. The three things about our marriage relationship that are *good* are ———.

13. The three things about our marriage relationship right now that are *great* are ———.

If you have a difficult time trying to determine your marital strengths, you may be interested in the findings of Dr. Herbert Otto. In his book *More Joy in Your Marriage,* Dr. Otto lists twelve qualities commonly reported by many couples as their marital strengths.[6] While no couple would likely have all of these strengths, each couple probably has one or more. See if any of these strengths are, or could be, characteristic of your own marriage.

1. We observe certain traditions and rituals in our marriage by celebrating birthdays, anniversaries, holidays, and other special occasions together.

2. We become involved in organizations at the local, state, and national level that are identified with selected issues and concerns.

3. We foster curiosity and interest in each other by sharing such things as creative activities or reading materials. We also try new things together by initiating spontaneous and exciting endeavors.

4. We share recreational and educational pursuits by participating in fun games and sports. We also encourage each other in a variety of educational experiences.

5. We meet each other's emotional needs by creating a sensitivity for warmth, affection, love, and understanding.

6. We have a mutually satisfying sexual relationship and enjoy lovemaking together, thereby deriving mutual enhancement from physical intimacy.

7. We have and enjoy a network of friends and relatives whose presence we enjoy individually and together.

8. We openly communicate with each other by being honest when sharing our feelings and thoughts in a sensitive way.

9. We have and share a spiritual life together by seeking deep and meaningful spiritual experiences individually, as a couple, and collectively in a religious community.

10. We give frequent support to each other through mutual caring to help confront our many details, tasks, chores, and other major responsibilities.

11. We have organizational efficiency as a couple which enables us to plan and carry out a variety of tasks and responsibilities.

12. We have role flexibility so husband and wife can assume some of each other's responsibilities according to needs and circumstances. Such flexibility allows for change, growth, and spontaneity.

If some of these aspects of your marriage could be improved, perhaps you and your partner could agree on one or more of them and work toward strengthening them during the coming year. It may be that you already enjoy the relationship you have. But we need to remember the 4-H motto: "To make the best better." And we ought not to fear change.

John Steinbeck wrote, "It is the nature of man as he grows older to protest against change, particularly change for the better." Similarly, Mignon McLaughlin noted, "It's the most unhappy people who most fear change."

Your Marriage Lifeline

Another way to gain perspective of your marriage and the maturation of your love is by doing an exercise called "Marriage Lifeline." It is from the book *I Need to Have You Know Me* by Roland and Doris Larson of Minneapolis, Minnesota.[7] This exercise will help you recall the times in your marriage when you have been very happy and felt close to each other.

Follow these instructions individually. Then share your responses with each other.

1. On a sheet of paper draw a straight horizontal line about six to eight inches long. This represents your marriage lifeline. At the left end of the line write the year you were married.

2. At the right end of the line, write a date when you and your partner might die. The year will be a guess, but it should be a realistic one in terms of what you know about the two of you. Most men live until their late sixties or early seventies. And most women live well into their seventies or early eighties.

3. Place an X somewhere on your marriage lifeline to represent the present year.

4. Now look at the left side of the line from the time of your marriage up until the present. What feelings and thoughts do those years represent? For each of the following events locate the approximate year on the lifeline and indicate it with the appropriate letter:

H= a very Happy experience you had together
T= an experience that brought you close Together
S= a period of Stress
C= the year your first Child arrived, or the year you plan to have a child.

5. Now look at the X on the marriage lifeline and move your eyes toward the future. What in five or ten years from now is fairly predictable? A job change? Children leaving home? Paying off a debt or mortgage? Buying a new home? Substantial changes in your life? Record these events somewhere near the appropriate spot on your future marital lifeline.

Now you are ready to share items 1-5 with your partner. As you do so, you should learn more about each other and your marriage. But to learn, you need to listen to each other and encourage each other to talk about what you have written. One way to do this is to ask clarifying questions such as "Can you tell me more about . . . ?" Or, "When did you first discover . . . ?" Or you might ask questions such as "How do you feel about that now?" Invent your own questions by trying to focus on the other person so he or she will want to respond to your questions.

It is wise, on occasion, for husbands and wives to look back over what they have experienced and perhaps endured in marriage over the years. More importantly, however, couples should also look toward the future and not only anticipate but also plan for some fulfilling and good times together to nurture their love.

Perhaps your marriage has been less than fulfilling in the past. But the past must no longer be used as an anvil for beating out the present and the future. Regardless of previous experiences, each couple has differing amounts of time left together in their marriage to learn to love. Some have decades, while others may have years, months, or only weeks. The point is that all married couples have *some* time left to plan and share. And we should make the most of that time, no matter how long it is.

Albert Schweitzer once wrote, "The tragedy of man is not that man dies, but what dies within man while he is living." If we work hard at developing love in our marriage, the present can become the good old days that the next generation will hear so much about in the future.

A Truly Happy Marriage

I was talking to a friend recently, and she posed a question I could not answer: "Just how many people are happily married nowadays?"

Most of us are realistic enough to know that not everyone who stays married is necessarily happy. One national study indicated that 80 percent of the married couples surveyed stated that under the same circumstances they would marry the same person again.

Whether or not this particular sample was truly representative is not known. But it does reflect similar findings of a study done in Ohio a few years ago.

John Cuber and Peggy Harroff interviewed nearly five hundred married people and from those discussions derived the following classifications and percentages: vital marriages (17 percent), congenial marriages (33 percent), devitalized marriages (33 percent), and combative marriages (17 percent).[8]

The vital marriages were those in which the partners were truly significant to each other. They liked being together, enjoyed each other's company, and had much going for them in their relationship. People in vital marriages placed great emphasis on each other as individuals rather than the services they rendered to each other.

The congenial marriages were those in which the couples got along and had a few differences or confrontations, but the vitality present in the vital marriages was missing. The people in congenial marriages emphasized maintaining a well-functioning home so their family members could participate in their community, occupational, civic, or church activities. In congenial marriages a marriage partner often became a means to an end so the events in life could be dealt with in an orderly fashion.

The devitalized marriages were those where a married couple once had something of significance, perhaps vitality, but somewhere along the way they lost it. The difference between congenial and devitalized marriages was that the congenial marriages never had any vitality nor was it expected. Devitalized marriages, on the other hand, once had vitality but were not able to retain it. Some devitalized couples explained, "That's just the way life is."

The combative marriages were those in which frequent confrontations and arguments occurred. Such became the rule rather than the exception. The couples verbally assaulted each other, often for months on end. And couples in combative marriages seemed to thrive on the one-upmanship that was required to keep the confrontations constant.

It should be noted that in all four categories of marriage the couples were still together and had no immediate intentions of divorce. The couples preferred the type of relationship they had over divorce. Otherwise, they could have chosen separation as an option.

My friend and I decided that there are many kinds of happiness and many types of marriage. We can learn to tolerate a marriage partner much as we would tolerate an obnoxious guest, live together in serenity with nothing more in common than cell mates in prison, or develop a love relationship from which both partners can derive genuine satisfaction.

Perhaps I am an eternal optimist, but I believe the vast majority of married couples can be in the latter category if both partners choose to do so.

Maybe the grass does often look greener on the other side of the marital fence. But someone once observed that the grass is greener where you water it.

How Do You Keep Your Marriage Vital?

John Cuber and Peggy Harroff noted in their study the phenomenon that the vitality once present in many marriages has either diminished or is missing altogether.

Almost all marriages start out with a high degree of hope, enthusiasm, optimism, and vitality. As young couples repeat their vows on their wedding day they epitomize such love and commitment.

But, as Cuber and Harroff observed, something happens to many couples along the marital path. For one thing, it is very difficult to maintain the high degree of personal attention and romantic involvement that brought the couple together. The authors call this loss of attentiveness and interest "devitalization."

The same study indicated that devitalization in marriage is usually dealt with in one of two ways. First, as previously noted, the couples may accept it as a fact of life. To them, that is just how marriage is supposed to be. Jobs, children, and outside activities such as excessive community and church involvement often become so demanding that the marriage has to be put on the back burner while either or both spouses try to meet these many obligations. Such couples usually do little to try and change the events, trends, or priorities.

The other way couples confront devitalization in marriage, according to Cuber and Harroff, is to guard against it. Even though the vast majority of married couples experience some degree of devitalization, many are not content to let their marital relationships give way to the daily demands of life. Such couples make conscious and often creative efforts to keep each other first, even though it means making some concessions or even sacrifices in other areas. Such endeavors usually turn out to be preventative rather than corrective in nature.

Has your marriage become devitalized? If so, are you accepting or fighting the devitalization? Think about it.

On a similar note, Dick and Paula McDonald have written a book called *Loving Free*. In it they note, "Boring, stale, deadly, dull, stagnant—these are words that we use to describe books, breads, ponds, and people. Occasionally those same words can be applied to marriage."[9]

The McDonalds caution, "To assure that a relationship stays alive and vital, the two people concerned have to actively look for ways to keep themselves interesting and retain the electricity in their lives together."

Many marriages in the United States lose the original zest the bride and groom seemed to have at the beginning of the marriage. The McDonalds ask them,

> Remember when you two began dating and were eager to share everything? You never wanted to go home no matter how late the hour, because you had a genuine desire to learn as much as you could about each other. Time flew by. You didn't feel tired nor were you ever bored with each other. And you never seemed to run out of things to discuss. . . .
>
> Those were the days when all of us were actively reaching out to know each other and to be close. Did we quit growing because it took away time from our babies and from our heavy work schedule? Did we stop trying to learn about each other because we thought we knew everything—or knew enough? When that day comes in marriage, boredom sets in, and your life together can become nothing more than a sad, lonely ritual, a prison for two people tied together by familiarity, children, and possessions.

As I talk to numerous married couples of various ages, I am impressed with the efforts so many have made to keep their love and marriage vital and alive.

I once wrote a column in the *Deseret News* about the importance of keeping a marriage alive and vital. I asked readers to write and tell me ways they have kept the zip in their marriage over the years.

I received 140 letters with some good ideas. The vast majority said they simply got away for a few days WC (Without Children!). Some took a short vacation (a second honeymoon, it was often called), went camping, or drove to a nearby city for a day or two of rest in a hotel or motel. Others indicated they did not go on or could not afford extended two- or three-day trips but periodically went out together.

Many others simply arranged to spend time together at home, often after the children had gone to bed, to talk and spend some time in mutual activity such as reading, playing card games, or any general activity where they were in each other's presence alone.

Several other activities were mentioned, such as prayer, weekly devotionals, and church attendance, to increase the overall spiritual dimensions of the marriage and the home.

Other joint activities included daily walks or jogging together, participating in dancing or study groups, playing racquetball or tennis, modifying (increasing or decreasing) community and church activities, increasing the frequency of touch, giving backrubs, and making a conscious effort to improve their sexual relationship.

Following is one letter typical of the 140 I received:

Dear Dr. Barlow:

I found your article on vitalizing your marriage interesting. Not only was it our fourth anniversary, but my best friend just announced that she and her husband are getting divorced. It caused me to think.

We haven't done any one big thing to revitalize our relationship, but we have done several small ones. First, we try to keep communication channels open. This can be difficult at times. But sometimes I just leave small notes around the house to surprise my husband.

Frequently we go out. We leave our son with a babysitter and have made it a policy to leave our household problems at home and not discuss them while we are gone. We spend the evening talking about mutual interests, much as we did when we were dating.

I have begun to develop my interests so I can talk to him about things outside our home. We have also tried to keep our sex life alive. We are open about our affection for each other and find it easy to discuss these matters.

Above all, we try to keep each other in the highest esteem. We care about each other and emphasize loyalty. And our relationship is treasured above all else and above all others.

One wife, however, gave the following caution:

I wonder sometimes if we expect too much excitement in marriage. As Archie Bunker once said to Edith, "Bein' bored is an important part of bein' married." I am not saying that we should not try to keep marriage interesting and exciting at times. But I really feel that some couples expect too much. Perhaps we need to learn to enjoy the simple things in life and not expect too much excitement. Excessively high expectations in marriage put a lot of pressure on both husbands and wives.

She then enclosed the following beautiful excerpt about love from the book *War Within and Without* by Anne Morrow Lindbergh:

Charles is gone again. The three days when he was here were so full and intense it seems they weighed more than the days before or after. And it is difficult to record them. They had that kind of premarriage intensity and preciousness that is difficult to capture. With the dull pain of departure—like a threatening thunderstorm over an afternoon—the light is more beautiful on an afternoon like that. The green is more green, the earth more vivid. But this is an unreal light.

These days are not marriage. They are being in love, but not the casual give and take, the wonderful blending of silence and communication, sharing and solitariness, being bored and being stimulated, disputes and agreements, the everyday and the extraordinary, the near and the far—that wonderful blending that makes for the incredible richness, variety, harmoniousness, and toughness of marriage.

Marriage is tough, because it is woven of all these various elements, the weak and the strong. "In loveness" is fragile for it is woven only with the gossamer threads of beauty. It seems to me absurd to talk about "happy" and "unhappy" marriages. Real marriages are both at the same time. But if they are real marriages, they always have this incredible richness for which one is eternally joyful and grateful.

It is strange, I can conceive of "falling in love" over and over again. But marriage, this richness of life itself, I cannot conceive of having again—or with anyone else. In this sense marriage seems to me indissoluble.[10]

2

SPIRITUALITY

Something very significant to me as a Latter-day Saint is our claim that the restored gospel of Jesus Christ has the answers or solutions to life's problems. Among these many problems are those related to marriage and family life.

The Prophet Joseph Smith once remarked, "Happiness is the object and design of our existence; and will be the end thereof, if we pursue the path that leads to it; and this path is virtue, uprightness, faithfulness, holiness, and keeping all the commandments of God."[1]

Recently we have realized more than ever that human beings need social, emotional, and spiritual needs filled in order to survive. And many husbands indicated they expected their wives to help them attain their spiritual needs in order to be happy.

The Gospel Has the Answers

As early as 1920, Church leaders were teaching that "the gospel has the answers." During the April general conference of that year, Elder Stephen L Richards stated, "The gospel of Jesus Christ is the power of God unto salvation. . . . I believe that within the plan of the gospel are laid down all of the laws and principles that underlie our lives, here and hereafter. It sets forth a rule of action for our conduct that leads us to happiness and joy in this life, as well as to exaltation in the life to come."[2]

During that same conference, Elder David O. McKay stated, "I believe, too, that every *world problem may be solved by obedience to the principles of the gospel of Jesus Christ.*"[3]

On a similar theme, Elder Harold B. Lee later noted, "It is wonderful when we come to realize that within the revealed gospel of Jesus Christ and from the teachings of our Church leaders in this dispensation may be found the answer to every question and a solution to every problem essential to the social, temporal, and spiritual welfare of human beings, all of whom, of course, are the children of our Heavenly Father."[4]

And after becoming President of the Church, President Kimball stated, "We have the positive approach. We believe that we have in this church the answer to all the questions, for the Lord is the head of the church and He has given us this program. We believe that if you take the commandments and go right down from one to ten (Exodus 20:1-17) everyone will be furthered by living the commandments as we are teaching them. We feel that we have a program that will overcome the evils of the day."[5]

All of us who believe that the gospel has the answer to life's major problems have a major task ahead. And it will be at a time when there appears to be so much turmoil in the world in the areas of marriage and family. Elder David O. McKay noted, "The responsibility of showing to the world that the gospel of Jesus Christ will solve its problems rests upon the men [and women] who make the claim."[6]

A *Revelation to Wives*

If the gospel has the answers to marital problems, one would expect it to have a message for wives as well as husbands. The Lord gave at least some of this counsel in the twenty-fifth section of the Doctrine and Covenants. Most of us think of this section as the "hymnbook section," in which Emma Smith was counseled by the Lord to accumulate hymns to be used in the Church. (Verses 11-13.) Actually, this section contains much more than that. It is a revelation to Emma in particular and to all women in general.

(See D&C 25:16.) And much of the revelation is about a wife's relationship with her husband.

Among the things revealed to Emma were the following:

1. She should "murmur not." (Verse 4.) I don't know if women are more inclined to complain than men, but it is significant to me that women are cautioned about frequent complaints. When I have mentioned this to women, many of them remind me that there is a difference between murmuring and righteous concern. And they are correct. Wives should convey to husbands concerns they have about many matters. But to avoid the appearance of complaining, they should consider the timing, tone of voice, frequency, importance, and clarity of the concern they express to their husbands. (See chapter 6 on communication.)

2. Emma was encouraged to "be for a comfort" for her husband. (Verse 5.) It is also of interest that she was to do this during the times of his afflictions, using consoling words. Like wives, husbands often need to be nurtured during difficult moments. And marriage affords us many opportunities to render this service to one another.

3. Emma was counseled to "go with [Joseph] at the time of his going." (Verse 6.) This is particularly significant when we realize how often Joseph and Emma moved and the many trials and heartaches they suffered for the gospel's sake. At Brigham Young University I have the opportunity to talk to young wives whose husbands are about to graduate. Many of them are anxious about where they will move to find employment. Some are hesitant about moving away from family, friends, and familiar surroundings. We often read together the Lord's counsel to "go with him at the time of his going."

The ability of many husbands to provide for their families has been severely hampered by wives who are unwilling to move or stay moved once they arrive. Such attitudes sometimes add additional burdens to marriage.

4. Emma was counseled not to fear or worry. (Verse 9.) I firmly believe that wives are given the gift of concern about many

matters we husbands often overlook. But with that gift sometimes comes the inclination to worry excessively. Jesus taught us to live life from day to day and not become overly worried about things of the future: "Do not worry about tomorrow, for tomorrow will worry about itself. Each day has enough trouble of its own." (Matthew 6:34, New International Version.)

5. Emma was admonished to "lay aside the things of this world, and seek for the things of a better." (Verse 10.) In other words, Emma was to place emphasis on the spiritual rather than the temporal things of life. This is more difficult than it appears. Most women would like a better or newer home, better furniture, dishes, clothing, and other things for herself and her family. This is understood, normal, and largely a part of the culture we live in. Just listen to one night's advertising on television and read the ads in daily newspapers, and you will soon realize that the desire for new and better things does not always arise from within. Most husbands want their wives and children to have the best they can offer or provide. But some wives, often unknowingly, cause their husbands much mental anguish because they desire and seek the "things of this world" more rapidly than they can be provided. I know of many families who have almost gone under financially because the wives were so caught up in *keeping* up that no amount of resources could quench their desire for newer and better material things. The advice given to Emma and other wives a century and a half ago seems even more relevant today.

6. Finally, Emma was warned against pride or arrogance. (Verse 14.) I believe this is particularly important for contemporary women. Many wives have told me that they feel they have "outgrown" their husbands. Perhaps because I work in an educational setting, I frequently see a man working hard to provide for his wife and family while his wife continues her education. In most cases, this does not negatively affect the marriage.

But on occasion I have seen relationships in which the wife becomes well-educated and feels that her husband can no longer keep up with or appreciate her new views on life. (I also see this happen to husbands who attend graduate school, graduate, and then become arrogant and divorce their wives for similar reasons. While we were attending graduate school, my wife, Susan, informed me that if I ever left her after getting my Ph.D., she would personally track me down and dissect me in public!)

The simple truth is, both husbands and wives have strengths and weaknesses. And we should avoid assuming that we are more than or less than each other. Emma and all women were encouraged, "Let thy soul delight in thy husband." (Verse 14.) By diligently working at their relationship and keeping it high in priority, both husbands and wives can delight in each other.

The Ideal Wife

Additional insights for wives are also given in other scriptures. Some people think of the Bible as a dusty old book written thousands of years ago with no relevance for today. While it is true that some of the language may be antiquated, I am amazed at the relevance of most of the Bible teachings for contemporary life. Brigham Young once noted, "Follow out the doctrines of the Bible and men will make splendid husbands, women excellent wives, and children will be obedient."[7] In the Bible, then, are some guidelines for present-day marriage and family living. What are some of them for wives?

The book of Proverbs mentions an otherwise unidentified man named Lemuel. Like any other woman, Lemuel's mother was concerned about the kind of woman her son would someday marry. His choice, however, was particularly significant since one day he would become a king, and his wife, consequently, a queen, a thought that bears some significance for Latter-day Saints. What was his mother's advice? What kind of woman should Lemuel marry? What should a husband expect of a wife?

In the thirty-first chapter of Proverbs, Lemuel was admonished to find a woman who was virtuous (verse 10) and whom he could trust (verse 11). She should do good (verse 12) and be willing and able to work with her hands (verse 13). Lemuel was encouraged to find a woman who was knowledgeable about foods and willing to prepare and serve a variety of them to her household. (Verses 14-15.) The woman he was to marry should have some knowledge of purchasing land, which implies an understanding of money management and financing. She should also be familiar with agriculture in that she could plant and reap from her own vineyards. (Verse 16.)

Lemuel's wife was to be physically fit and healthy, even strong, in that she "girdeth her loins with strength, and strengtheneth her arms." (Verse 17.) She was to be knowledgeable in consumer economics and able to trade wisely. (Verse 18.) Not only that, she was expected to know how to produce some of her own goods without having to purchase all of them. (Verse 19.)

The new bride was expected to be charitable, with a genuine concern for the poor and needy. (Verse 20.) Her children were to be well-clothed and prepared for inclement weather. (Verse 21.) And she herself was to dress fashionably. (Verse 22.) She was to be supportive of her husband and to be cognizant of his reputation. (Verse 23.) She was encouraged to become involved in merchandising both in production and selling. (Verse 24.) And the woman Lemuel married was to be well-educated, in that she "openeth her mouth with wisdom." (Verse 26.) She was not to have a harsh tongue (verse 26), and was to be attentive to the needs of those in her household through her diligence (verse 27).

She should be honored and praised by her children and husband (verse 28) and excel in many aspects of life (verse 29). And perhaps most important, she was to be a woman who loved the Lord. (Verse 30.)

In capsule form, then, this is what many husbands, ancient and modern, expect of wives. And what a delight such a wife would be! Truly, "her price is far above rubies." (Verse 10.)

Loving Leadership in the Home

One of the recent criticisms of the current women's movement is that men have traditionally been "the head of the home," supposedly to the detriment of some women. Since the Church continues to teach, and I believe rightfully so, that the husband should provide the leadership in the home, we will likely continue to be criticized.

But it also concerns me that many men and women in the Church raise some question about the validity of the man presiding in the home in what we often call the patriarchal order of marriage. It may well be that such a marriage is the answer, or one of the answers, the restored gospel provides for stable marriages and family life.

A recent college textbook on marriage and family relations contained an interesting section called "The Peculiarities of American Marriage." Discussing the power structure of marriages, the author wrote, "One of the greatest peculiarities of American marriage, as compared to almost all other societies, is the relative dominance of the American wife."[8]

The recent transition in the United States from a patriarchal to a democratic or even a matriarchal family organization has had its consequences. Dr. Edward J. Rydman, past executive director of the American Association of Marriage and Family Counselors, noted:

> There has been a profound shift from the authoritarian family in which the husband-father had the major control over his wife and children. Most of the family power, decision-making responsibility, and authority rested upon him, as did the responsibility for supporting the family economically. The shift from the authoritarian to a more equalitarian family has profoundly affected the position of the head of the family as women have entered the economic marketplace in ever-increasing numbers and especially as even larger numbers of mothers take their place in offices, assembly lines, and other occupations and professions. As women assume more responsibilities outside the home so stresses, strains, and problems within the family relationship proliferate.[9]

The recent trend in family government is also a departure from biblical teachings. The apostle Paul admonished, "Wives, submit yourselves unto your own husbands." (Ephesians 5:22; see also Colossians 3:18.) He also taught that "the husband is the head of the wife." (Ephesians 5:23.) It is true that in some Latter-day Saint homes the wife or mother must assume a major portion of the responsibility in governing family affairs. Such would be the case, for example, if the father were absent because of death or divorce or if he were incapacitated through illness or injury. But what about Latter-day Saint homes where both father and mother are still together? What should be the relationship between a Latter-day Saint husband and wife, particularly if the husband holds the priesthood?

In 1902, shortly after becoming sixth president of the Church, President Joseph F. Smith stated:

> There is no higher authority in matters relating to the family organization, and especially when that organization is presided over by one holding the higher Priesthood, than that of the father. The authority is time honored, and among the people of God in all dispensations it has been highly respected and often emphasized by the teachings of the prophets who were inspired of God. *The patriarchal order is of divine origin and will continue throughout time and eternity.* There is, then, a particular reason why men, women and children should understand this order and this authority in the households of the people of God, and seek to make it what God intended it to be, a qualification and preparation for the highest exaltation of his children. In the home the presiding authority is always vested in the father, and in all home affairs and family matters there is no other authority paramount.[10] (Italics added.)

Do such teachings have relevance for contemporary Latter-day Saint marriages and families? Questions immediately arise as to how the patriarchal order operates in a Latter-day Saint home. Both the validity and the practical application of the principle need careful evaluation.

In what manner does a Latter-day Saint husband act as "head" over his wife? Must a woman "obey" her husband at all times in all things? Does a wife have any part in the decision-making policies in her marriage and family? (See chapter 6 on communication.) Is a patriarch similar to a dictator who rules with absolute control and often in a domineering way?

President Kimball once observed, "We have heard of men who have said to their wives, 'I hold the priesthood and you've got to do what I say.' Such a man should be tried for his membership.

Certainly he should not be honored in his priesthood. We rule (preside) in love and understanding."[11]

A Latter-day Saint husband or father presides over his wife and family in much the same way that a bishop, stake president, elders quorum president, Relief Society president or Primary president presides over the specific group to which he or she is called. Each acts with counselors and seldom makes decisions without carefully consulting those called to assist.

A counselor may be chosen to officiate in the absence of the appointed leader. Even in the presence of the leader, the counselor may conduct by appointment while the leader presides. In a similar manner, according to President Joseph F. Smith, "in the home the presiding authority is always vested in the father." He explained why:

> This patriarchal order has its divine spirit and purpose, and those who disregard it under one pretext or another are out of harmony with the spirit of God's laws as they are ordained for recognition in the home. It is not merely a question of who is perhaps the best qualified. Neither is it wholly a question of who is living the most worthy life. It is a question largely of law and order, and its importance is seen often from the fact that the authority remains and is respected long after a man is really unworthy to exercise it.[12]

Imagine the confusion that would result if two bishops were appointed over a ward and the first got up in sacrament meeting and announced that the following Sunday sacrament meeting would be held one hour earlier than usual. While he was making his announcement, suppose the second bishop stood up and expressed his desire that the meeting be held at the usual time. With two people presiding, would democratic principles work? Suppose you had two stake presidents, two elders quorum presidents, two Primary and Relief Society presidents presiding over each of the priesthood quorums, groups, or auxiliaries. How would the Church function? Would "law and order" prevail? Similarly, should two people preside over each other in a marriage, particularly when one holds the priesthood and has been divinely designated to preside?

We can better understand the similarity of presiding over a home or a ward by examining some of Paul's teachings. He taught that for a man to be ordained a bishop, he must be married and be "one that ruleth well his own house, having his children in subjection with all gravity." (1 Timothy 3:4.) He should have "faithful children not accused of riot or unruly." (Titus 1:6.)

By proving himself capable of presiding over his primary responsibility—his wife and family—a man could assume a second stewardship in the priesthood. Paul reasoned, "For if a man know not how to rule his own house, how shall he take care of the church of God?" (1 Timothy 3:5.)

Paul stated there was a "great mystery" associated with the patriarchal order. (See Ephesians 5:32.) The mystery may not be so much in the manner in which a wife submits herself to her husband as, in fact, the way a husband will preside over and interact with his wife and family. President Joseph F. Smith observed, "This authority carries with it a responsibility and a grave one, as well as its rights and privileges, and men can not be too exemplary in their lives, nor fit themselves too carefully to live in harmony with this important and God-ordained rule of conduct in the family organization."[13]

The apostle Paul urged, "Husbands, love your wives, even as Christ also loved the church, and gave himself for it. . . . So ought men to love their wives as their own bodies. He that loveth his wife loveth himself. For no man ever yet hated his own flesh; but nourisheth and cherisheth it, even as the Lord the church. . . . Let every one of you in particular so love his wife even as himself; and the wife see that she reverence her husband." (Ephesians 5:25, 28-29, 33.) Most wives would willingly submit to husbands who loved them in this manner.

Modern revelation declares how one holding the priesthood should officiate and preside, particularly over his wife and family. (See D&C 121:36-46.)

By strengthening the patriarchal order in Latter-day Saint homes, not only will the husband-wife relationship be enhanced, but the parent-child relationship will improve as well. When a wife challenges the right of her husband to officiate in the home, is it not a logical consequence that the children will challenge that right also? Furthermore, is it possible that a child will then not only challenge the right of the father but also that of the mother to make decisions affecting his life?

Again, Dr. Edward J. Rydman, the noted marriage counselor, has stated:

> Little scientific evidence is in at this time, but there is concern expressed in some quarters that the growing rebellion of youth is a logical extension of the shift toward equalitarianism. In a new way and in ever increasing numbers, the youth today are demanding a voice in education, marriage, sexual expression, and other significant areas of life. As woman challenges the authority of man, so youth challenges the authority of the family and all other related social institutions.[14]

Latter-day Saint parents may be facing a critical era. We have been commanded to teach our children gospel principles, to have faith in Christ, to repent, and to be baptized and receive the Holy Ghost. In essence, parents should "teach their children to pray, and to walk uprightly before the Lord." (D&C 68:28.) Failure to do these things has its consequences.

Paul also taught that "in the last days perilous times shall come. For [children] shall be . . . disobedient to parents, unthankful, unholy." (2 Timothy 3:1-2.) If Latter-day Saint families are going to survive the last days of "disobedience," we need to carefully examine those principles by which our families are governed and maintained.

The Lord commanded ancient Israel to "honour thy father and thy mother" (Exodus 20:12), a principle to be taught not only to children but to be demonstrated by the mother honoring the father as head of the household, and the father, in turn, honoring the mother.

When a husband and wife show honor and respect for each other, their children learn through their example to honor their parents. The commandment to honor father and mother, according to President Joseph F. Smith, is binding upon every member of the Church today, for the law is eternal.

If the patriarchal order of marriage is practiced as outlined by Church leaders and the scriptures, there is little question that Latter-day Saint husbands and wives will experience happier, more stable and satisfactory marriages. Furthermore, important guidelines for raising children can be used effectively in such a relationship. President Smith admonished:

> Wives and children should be taught to feel that the patriarchal order in the kingdom of God has been established for a wise and beneficent purpose, and should sustain the head of the household and encourage him in the discharge of his duties, and do all in their power to aid him in the exercise of the rights and privileges which God has bestowed upon the head of the home. . . .
>
> The necessity, then, of organizing the patriarchal order and authority of the home rests upon principle as well as upon the person who holds that authority, and among the Latter-day Saints family discipline, founded upon the law of the patriarchs, should be carefully cultivated, and fathers will then be able to remove many of the difficulties that now weaken their position in the home.[15]

Additional insights on the patriarchal order of marriage were recently given by Elder Dean L. Larsen of the Presidency of the First Quorum of the Seventy. His excellent article "Marriage and the Patriarchal Order" was printed in the *Ensign*, September 1982, pages 6-13. I think every Latter-day Saint husband and wife should read and reread the entire article. In it he notes:

> A superficial reading of the Old Testament account can easily leave one with the feeling that women were the property of men, consigned simply to do the bidding of their husbands and masters. There was much about the culture and the customs of ancient Israel that contributed to this general impression, and occasionally we encounter men of our own time who have allowed their knowledge of those ancient customs to influence their view of the patriarchal order.

Elder Larsen continues:

> One whose views of the husband-wife relationship is based upon the prevailing customs and culture of the Old Testament people is capable of creating much unhappiness for himself, his wife, and family. To qualify his view, he

should give careful consideration to the counsel of prophetic leaders who have taken pains to instruct us correctly in these matters. [For instance, see "In the Image of God," by President Marion G. Romney, *Ensign*, March 1978, pages 2-4.]

Elder Larsen encourages Latter-day Saint husbands and wives to carefully study Doctrine & Covenants 107:27-30 as a model for making decisions together in marriage and then gives a final admonition that goes hand-in-hand with the theme of this book. He writes: "I am convinced that there is something so absolutely sacred in the eyes of the Lord about the marriage covenant that he expects every energy and resource in our power to make our marriage endure. For those who do, even in the face of great challenges and difficulties, I am certain there will be ultimate blessings realized that are beyond our present comprehension."

A *Prayer of Love*

One of the teachings of our Church is, "If there is anything virtuous, lovely, or of good report or praiseworthy, we seek after these things." (Article of Faith 13.) During the past few years it has been my distinct pleasure to review many articles and books by numerous religious leaders that are praiseworthy and of good report. For example, a statement of love and commitment was written by Reverend Larry Hof and William R. Miller for married couples and was sponsored, in part, by the Saint Andrew's United Methodist Church and the Marriage Council of Philadelphia. The sentiments, I believe, should also be considered by Latter-day Saints. They are:

> Our marriage is not a finished product. It is an experience, a relationship that is being created continually. It is an ongoing process to which we must commit ourselves each day, making again the decision to share life together. The vows we have made serve as a reminder to us that in the midst of all the possibilities of separation which are open to us, we have decided again to be faithful to the commitment which we have made to each other in the presence of God.[16]

Hof and Miller also wrote this prayer of love:

Dear God:

I give to my husband/wife a love that, in the words of Paul, is patient, a love that is kind, a love that endures. I pledge a love that is not jealous or possessive, a love that is not proud or selfish, a love that is not rude or inconsiderate. My love will not insist on its own way, will not be irritable or resentful, and will not keep account of wrongs or failures. It will rejoice when good prevails. Our love will know no limit to its endurance, no end to its trust, no fading of its hope. It will outlast everything. Our love together, will have three great qualities: faith . . . hope . . . and love, but the greatest of these will be our love for each other. In the name of Him who embodies love, Jesus Christ, Amen. (See 1 Corinthians 13:4-13.)[17]

One of my favorite biblical passages is 1 John 4:7-11. John could have been speaking to married couples when he wrote:

Beloved, let us love one another: for love is of God; and every one that loveth is born of God, and knoweth God. He that loveth not knoweth not God; for God is love. In this was manifested the love of God toward us, because that God sent his only begotten Son into the world, that we might live through him. Herein is love, not that we loved God, but that he loved us, and sent his Son to be the propitiation for our sins. Beloved, if God so loved us, we ought also to love one another.

In an age of uncertainty, particularly in the realm of marriage, husbands and wives seem to be searching for something on which they can build a solid foundation in their relationship. And learning to love one another, as outlined in the scriptures, is the answer. Through the ages we have been told, "Charity [love] never faileth." (1 Corinthians 13:8; Moroni 7:46.)

3

SUPPORT

Wives should be aware that their husbands want and need support. In the questionnaire "Understanding Your Expectations" (appendix A), the item "She supports me in my endeavors both at home and at work" was ranked very high by many husbands in my survey. In fact, support was ranked third.

I do not believe that a husband's ego is necessarily more vulnerable than his wife's. In *What Wives Expect of Husbands,* women indicated that they need sensitivity, which may be another way of saying they need support. Rather than argue whether husbands or wives need support the most, we may simply conclude that all people need support, encouragement, sensitivity, and appreciation.

Remember the Lord's counsel to Emma Smith to be "a comfort unto my servant, Joseph Smith, Jun., thy husband, in his afflictions, with consoling words, in the spirit of meekness." (D&C 25:5.) Perhaps because of his awareness that married couples would undergo great stress in the latter days, the Lord encouraged husbands and wives to love and nurture one another.

Tough Times for Husbands

I do think these are tough times for many husbands. In his book *Parents in Modern America,* E. E. LeMasters has written a chapter entitled "The American Father."[1] In it he documents some of the serious problems of fathers and husbands:

1. *Economic problems.* Although most husbands and fathers are relatively well off by many standards, most husbands are under constant economic pressure to support a wife and children. This is particularly true with the constant bombardment from the media that the family must continually have "more and better" things. Note the huge increase in consumer credit during the past few years or the personal bankruptcy notices in the daily paper.

For the 20 to 30 percent of husbands and fathers who are in the lower levels of the economic system, financial problems are even more of a reality. According to LeMasters, such husbands are faced not only with the daily realities of being able to provide food, clothing, and housing for their families, but with the knowledge that in a society in which many are reasonably well off, they are not.

LeMasters believes, however, that almost all husbands presently suffer from economic problems of one kind or another. If the problem is not how to get enough money, it is often what to do with it or how to hold on to it. He concludes, "Only those who have sweated out economic problems know how they can affect family life; the quality of the husband-wife relationship, the feeling of the children for their parents, and the attitude of the father and mother towards being parents. *A man's self-image in our society is deeply affected by his ability to provide for his family. Many times, the self-image is not too positive.*"[2] (Italics added.)

2. *Marital problems.* When a husband experiences conflict or turmoil in his marriage, it also affects many other things such as his work, his role as father, and his relationship with others. Marital tensions for husbands, and wives for that matter, are enormous at the present time, with some 40 percent of marriages ending in divorce and with some couples choosing to stay married in what LeMasters and others term "holy deadlock."

Many wives, I believe, are not fully aware of the degree to which they can bless or burden a husband in his activities. Latter-day revelation urges wives to "murmur not." (D&C 25:4.) And with regard to financial matters, wives have been counseled to "lay aside the things of this world." (D&C 25:10.)

Some wives live for many years with the illusion that nothing is wrong with their relationship. Then after several years of married life, they find themselves seriously contemplating divorce. A student of mine came by my office recently and wanted to talk for a few minutes. He was a handsome young man and appeared to be very intelligent. And he was concerned. He told me that after nearly thirty years of marriage, his parents were getting a divorce.

As we sat in my office that morning, he reflected, "It is one thing to get a divorce after several years of struggling with a bad relationship. But my parents had a picture-perfect marriage all the years I was growing up. We had a large family, a hard-working father, and a sensitive, concerned mother, and all of us regularly participated in church activities. How could a divorce happen?"

I've had that kind of conversation more than once during the past few years. Young men and women about to marry find their parents seeking a divorce. The separations occur after what appeared to be ideal marital relationships. And the question is asked time and time again: Why?

I told the young man that I did not know the reasons why picture-perfect marriages sometimes come unframed. But I am starting to form some opinions. And my opinions are centered around the picture-perfect marriage concept. Many believe, or are misled to believe, that they have an ideal marriage. Since they now have it, they may think they don't have to do anything to keep it. And that just may make the difference.

During the past few years, I have participated in several marriage education seminars. It is refreshing to meet with many couples who are deeply committed to marriage. During these seminars, however, I did not find picture-perfect marriages. What I did find were couples of all ages who deeply loved each other and were consequently willing to struggle together to keep their good marriages functioning.

Someone once observed that it is better to have a heart attack and then learn to take care of your health than to live without knowing you have heart problems. So it is with marriage. Working to improve a somewhat less-than-perfect marriage may be far better than living under the illusion that we have the ideal marital relationship.

3. *Sexual problems.* Because sexual fulfillment is such an important part of masculinity for husbands, sexual problems and disruptions can be a major source of frustration for them. In his chapter "The American Father," LeMasters notes that men are expected to find sexual fulfillment with their marriage partners. Many do. Some do not.

When sexual disruption occurs at home, some husbands feel they have the right to seek elsewhere for sexual fulfillment, and sexual fidelity in marriage appears to be decreasing in the United States and other places.

LeMasters does not, nor do I, condone the intentions or actions of men seeking sexual fulfillment outside of marriage. Husbands and wives share a joint responsibility to fulfill each other's sexual needs. If husbands do not receive sexual fulfillment or if they are unfaithful, according to LeMasters, their role as fathers or husbands will suffer.

4. *Drinking and drug-related problems.* Under stress, an increasing number of husbands and fathers turn to alcohol or other drugs as an escape. LeMasters notes that men are three to six times more likely to drink alcohol excessively in our society than are women.

When a husband and father drinks, it affects his family in at least four ways: (1) the drinking becomes a real strain on the family budget; (2) the quality of the marriage almost always suffers; (3) when the husband is at home he is not able to function normally—he is either too good to the children or he is abusive; and (4) the attitude of his children and his wife usually changes from positive to negative. Perhaps similar trends occur with the misuse of other drugs.

5. *The male peer problem.* LeMasters notes that husbands need and seek the company of other men during much of their spare time. While this is widely accepted, it has caused some problems. A great many women view marriage and parenthood as a joint partnership and do not readily accept "male only" activities. In the past, men have preferred to spend some of their leisure time with other men, and giving up these associations can cause strain. If a wife refuses to make any concessions while the husband demands "the night or weekend with the boys," problems abound. On this matter, LeMasters concludes, "To resolve this sort of strain the American male has to be domesticated more than he ever has in the past. To what extent this has been accomplished, or can be accomplished, we don't know. But some men are difficult to harness, as their wives have discovered. When this is the case it seems likely that the father's (and husband's) role is diminished or affected negatively in some way."[3]

Some wives resent husbands who want time away from home and family for even a short period of time. I would remind such wives that in my book *What Wives Expect of Husbands* one frequent expectation of wives was autonomy. Wives wanted and expected time alone or in the company of friends. I believe that what is good for the goose is also good for the gander. Apparently, both husbands and wives need a periodic break to be alone with others.

Husbands Change

If you are not convinced by now that husbands need support, you may want to consider the thoughts of Dr. Joyce Brothers. Dr. Brothers, a noted psychologist, recently wrote the book *What Every Woman Should Know about Men.* In it she has several pages on "The Fragile Sex," documenting the many differences between men and women and the ways that men are often more vulnerable. And she also notes that men pass through several stages of life. She writes:

> In recent decades so much attention has been lavished on the stages of childhood—from the terrible twos through the teenage tyrants—that the adult

> st completely ignored. It was as if once a boy emerged from was a man and that was that and nothing much more hap- gan the inevitable descent into old age. True, every woman knew that a man in his forties was almost as unpredictable as an adolescent. But that was about it. No one paid much attention to the years between twenty and seventy-five.[4]

Dr. Brothers notes that times have changed and that many professionals have turned their attention to the adult male. They have discovered that men go through at least five stages with the first and third stages being the most crucial as well as the most difficult. These are:

Stage 1: *Onward and Upward.* These tension-ridden years are from about age twenty-one to about thirty-five. During this time a man concentrates on establishing himself at work, marrying, and starting a family.

Stage 2: *Consolidation.* This period lasts from the mid-thirties to the mid-forties and is the time when a man pulls together the accomplishments of the previous period.

Stage 3: *The Pivotal Decade.* During this time, which occurs from the mid-forties to the mid-fifties, a man senses the arrival of middle age, which is usually characterized by physical and psychological stress as he reorients himself. Dr. Brothers believes that the quality and character of the rest of a man's life are largely determined during this pivotal decade.

Stage 4: *Equilibrium.* From the mid-fifties until retirement a man goes through the years of equilibrium, which can be very rewarding. Problems not resolved during the Pivotal Decade can carry over into this stage, which may prolong the Pivotal Decade and shorten the Equilibrium Stage.

Stage 5: *Retirement.* Depending on what happens during the Pivotal Decade and the Equilibrium stage, this fifth stage can be a time of major satisfaction and serenity. Or, it can be a time of resentment, disappointment, and fear.

Dr. Brothers believes that the woman who understands what a man is going through during these different stages will be able to better deal with her husband as he passes through them. Or at least she may be able to cope more easily with the behavior changes and mood swings as he goes from one stage to the next. Husbands need particular support during stages 1 and 3 but evidently need it in one form or another throughout the years of marriage.

The Middle Years

My wife, Susan, and I have been confused trying to determine when the middle years are. The United States Census Bureau has defined the middle years as those between thirty-five and fifty-five, and yet another research project suggested that the middle years were those between fifty-five and seventy-five.

The logical conclusion could be drawn that anyone over thirty and under seventy-five is middle aged, but this is not necessarily so. One investigation of people over eighty years of age found that only half of them reported themselves as being old, and the other half defined themselves as being in the middle years of life. So if you are between thirty and somewhere near eighty years of age, you are in the middle years.

According to Dr. Joyce Brothers, the middle years are critical for husbands. And apparently that is where Susan and I are right now. Like most married couples we experience our moments of identity crisis. This happened not long ago when we realized we were no longer young but were not yet willing to concede that we were really old. We finally came to the rather logical conclusion that we are experiencing the middle years of marriage.

Trapped somewhere between puberty and paralysis, other married couples like ourselves may also be facing similar situations and asking some of the same questions. Having spent our youth, must we be reconciled to the idea that the best of life and marriage is over? Or, is it possible that the most rewarding part of marriage is yet ahead? Are those of us in the middle years of marriage approaching the summit, or are we over the hill?

What do the middle years hold for marriage? Some research indicates that the middle years are a time of challenge, frustration, transition, and change. Many middle-aged people report feeling caught and pressured. Economists have described the tremendous financial pressures on middle-aged couples. All of these thoughts would lead us to believe we are on the other side of the mountain longingly looking back at better times. While these trends may be true for some married couples, they need not be for all.

Dr. Richard Kerckhoff of Purdue University recently noted that the middle years of marriage can be, and often are, the best. According to Dr. Kerckhoff, they can be a time of recognition of our value, not a time to doubt our worth. The middle years can be a time of reassessment, of withdrawal from energy-consuming activities to which we were never really committed.

Dr. Kerckhoff suggests that during this time in our marriage we focus on the things we now feel are really worthwhile.[5]

The Four Cs of Support

Since husbands do need support, how might it be given? This is a logical question most wives may ask. Of course, husbands may differ in the amount and kind of support they need, so before trying to give specifics, I might suggest four general roles a wife might play to support her husband. They all start with the letter c.

Confidante. Almost all husbands want someone with whom they can share their deepest thoughts and innermost secrets. Every husband needs one person to whom he can open his heart, mind, and dreams. Such confidence usually tends to draw a husband and wife closer to each other.

Companion. A husband needs friends, and a wife ought to be his very best one. The Lord said, "It is not good that . . . man should be alone." (Genesis 2:18.) A husband needs someone he can talk to, someone who will listen to him and keep his confidences, and someone to accompany him through life.

One of the frequent complaints of husbands is that wives talk too much and do not listen enough. Many extramarital affairs begin because a man finds someone other than his wife who will listen to him when his wife won't. This listening turns to empathy, empathy to sympathy, and sympathy to desire. Such a woman, who may not necessarily be physically attractive, actively listens and by so doing wins the man's heart. If wives want their husbands to be faithful to them, they should learn to listen to them in a sympathetic way.

Conscience. A husband needs a wife he can trust and with whom he can clarify some of his thoughts. In my own marriage I have had ideas that needed clarification, review, or revising. My wife, Susan, is my contact with reality and in many ways my social conscience. Often in writing my column for the *Deseret News*, I will have some idea or thought that may be controversial or could be misunderstood. I will share the idea with her, and I know what she will say in advance: "When in doubt, leave it out!" Her philosophy has spared me much misunderstanding in my writing. And when I give a talk to a group or audience, I know I can trust her judgment on how well I have or have not done. I have benefited in many ways because Susan knows that I, like the vast majority of husbands, need another conscience, one who will help me with my thoughts and actions. Hopefully, I can do the same for her in some small way.

Climate controller. There is little question in my mind that the wife sets the general tone or climate of the home. And husbands appreciate and want wives who can help make this climate positive and pleasant. Because wives are around their children so much more than husbands, I believe they determine much of the atmosphere in which their children thrive and live. Of course, they are not totally responsible. But the simple fact is that women can and do accomplish much in creating the environment in the home.

A Crucial Question

While these are general ways wives might support their husbands, you may want to ask your own husband this crucial question: "How might I be more supportive of you as a husband and father?" Then, be willing to listen. You may be surprised and even informed.

One husband wrote:

I think it is imperative that my wife supports me at home as well as at other places, because if she has an apathetic attitude, it is most likely that her attitude will rub off on me. Sometimes I think, "If she doesn't care then why should I?"

Support from a wife can come in many ways. It might be a simple "How was your day, dear?" But it shouldn't stop there. She should continue to ask him questions to find out what really went on. If he had a bad day, maybe she can help him realize it wasn't quite so bad. If it was a good day, she should ask questions about that too.

I really feel my wife's support when she gets out of bed and sees me off to work in the morning. I appreciate it when she fixes my breakfast. One of my friends leaves for work every morning after a dish of cold cereal while his wife lies in bed. I know how he feels about it too, and he doesn't feel good.

A wife can also show support for her husband through touch. Even though we won't admit it, men need and want to be touched as much as do women.

In summary, one of the most effective and painless ways to strengthen your marriage is to find out how you can better support your husband and then do it.

4

MOTHERHOOD

Apparently the vast majority of husbands feel that the roles of wife and mother are intertwined. It is very difficult to separate marriage from parenthood and family. They all affect each other and are interrelated. But the fact remains that a woman can be a better mother than wife, and vice versa, depending on which role she gives top priority. Most do adequately at both.

Most husbands expect their wives to be competent mothers. Of the twenty items in appendix B, "She gives our children adequate emotional and physical care" was ranked fourth by husbands. A wife should realize, therefore, that how she functions as a mother will also affect her marriage.

Discipline

One of the scriptures that most interests me indicates that in the last days children will be disobedient to parents. (See 2 Timothy 3:2.) And we may now be observing this signs of the times. While both fathers and mothers contribute to the discipline of children, or lack of it, mothers are usually with the children much more often than are fathers. What mothers do, therefore, or fail to do to discipline is of major importance.

All too frequently discipline comes in the form of "Wait until your father gets home," which takes the responsibility of disciplining away from the mother and unduly burdens the father. Both husbands and wives need to help discipline their children.

In his popular book *Dare to Discipline,* Dr. James Dobson notes:

> Methods and philosophies regarding control of children have been the subject of heated debates and disagreements for centuries. The pendulum has swept back and forth regularly between harsh, oppressive discipline and the unstructured permissiveness of the 1950's. It is time that we realize that both extremes leave their characteristic scars on the lives of young victims, and I would be hard pressed to say which is more damaging.
>
> Unfortunately, the prevailing philosophy at a particular time seems to be more influential on parental approaches to discipline than does common sense.[1]

Elsewhere in his book, Dr. Dobson observes:

> Love in the absence of instruction will not produce a child with self-discipline, self-control, and respect for his fellow man. Affection and warmth underlie all mental and physical health, yet they do not eliminate the need for careful training and guidance. The greatest social disaster of this century is the belief that abundant love makes discipline unnecessary. Respectful and responsible children result from families where the proper combination of love and discipline is present. Both these ingredients must be applied in necessary quantities.[2]

Dr. Dobson then gives five major guidelines he believes are essential in teaching children self-control:

> 1. Discipline can only be effectively taught when there is mutual respect between parent and child.
> 2. Take the opportunity for communication and discussion with a child after a child has been disciplined.
> 3. Exert control over your children without nagging or continual reminding.
> 4. Don't saturate your child with excessive materialism or "things."
> 5. Avoid extremes in the application of both love and control.[3]

In marriage and family seminars I am frequently asked about spanking as a means of disciplining children. I reply that if spanking is the only means by which you can control your children, then do it. But frankly, Susan and I have found spanking to be quite ineffective in changing the behavior of our children. It seldom has positive long-range consequences.

Many people equate non-spanking with non-discipline, and for some parents that may be true. But there are other, more effective ways to discipline a child without having to spank.

Brigham Young once stated:

> Kind words and loving actions towards children, will subdue their uneducated natures a great deal better than the rod, or, in other words, than physical punishment. Although it is written that, "The rod and reproof give wisdom, but a child left to himself bringeth his mother to shame," [Proverbs 29: 15] and, "he that spareth his rod hateth his son; but he that loveth him chasteneth him betimes;" [Proverbs 13:24] these quotations refer to wise and prudent corrections. Children who have lived in the sunbeams of parental kindness and affection, when made aware of parent's displeasure, and receive a kind reproof from parental lips, are more thoroughly chastened, than by any physical punishment that could be applied to their persons. . . . When children are reared under the rod, . . . it not unfrequently occurs, that they become so stupefied and lost to every high-toned feeling and sentiment, that though you bray them in a mortar among wheat with a pestle, yet will not their foolishness depart from them.[4]

One of the best insights I have found on parent-child relationships is found in Doctrine and Covenants 121:43: "Reproving betimes with sharpness, when moved upon by the Holy Ghost; and then showing forth afterwards an increase of love toward him whom thou hast reproved, lest he esteem thee to be his enemy."

This revelation suggests that we should reprove or chastise clearly, concisely, and betimes (quickly) when moved upon by the Holy Ghost. The Holy Ghost will be our guide. Then our discipline will be controlled and consistent. (Remember that Jesus braided a whip before he cleansed the temple. You can crochet or do a little needlepoint before you are tempted to let your child have it!)

After reproving your child, be sure to show him an increase of love, "lest he esteem thee to be his enemy."

I know, as do many parents, what it means to be esteemed as

an enemy. But if there has been one thing I have constantly tried to do, it is to show an increase of love after discipline. And in so doing I have learned the power of that scripture.

How to Survive as a Mother

Dr. Dobson also notes:

> It is not uncommon for a mother . . . to feel overwhelmed by the complexity of her parental assignment. For each child she raises, she is the primary protector of his health, education, intellect, personality, character, and emotional stability. She must serve as physician, nurse, psychologist, teacher, minister, cook, and policeman. Since she is with the children longer each day than her husband, she is the chief disciplinarian and main giver of security and love. She will not know whether or not she is handling these matters properly until it is too late to change her methodology.
>
> Furthermore, Mom's responsibilities extend far beyond her children. She must also meet her obligations to her husband, her church, her relatives, her friends, and in some cases her employer. Each of these areas demands her best effort, and the conscientious mother often finds herself racing through the day in a breathless attempt to be all things to all people. . . . Certainly there must be occasions in the life of every mother when she looks in the mirror and asks, "How can I make it through the day?"

To help mothers "make it through the day," Dr. Dobson suggests the following:

1. *Reserve some time for yourself.* At least once a week spend a few hours on yourself or simply "waste" an occasional afternoon.

2. *Don't struggle with things you cannot change.* While a mother does make a difference in her children's lives and that of her husband, there are some things she just can't do or change. One of the first principles of mental health is to learn to accept the inevitable.

3. *Don't deal with any big problems late at night.* (This includes husband-wife relationships as well.) When we are fatigued and tired, our tolerance level is usually low. Much tension and hostility can be avoided by simply delaying important topics until morning. A good night's sleep can go a long way in defusing a problem.

4. *Write down a list of duties to be performed.* This will help remind you of your most important tasks. In addition, you can then set priorities for your items and start on those that seem to be most important. Then, at the end of the day, you can look back at the list and have the satisfaction of knowing you did one, two, or perhaps more of the things you decided were important.

5. *Seek divine assistance.* Dr. Dobson, a devout Christian, notes: "The concept of marriage and parenthood were not human inventions. God in His infinite wisdom, created and ordained the family as the basic unit of procreation and companionship. The solutions to the problems of modern parenthood can be found through the power of prayer and personal appeal to the Great Creator."[5]

You Have to Grow with Your Children

Someone once noted that rearing children is like making pancakes—you have to practice on the first one. Most parents readily concede that we practice becoming fathers and mothers on our first child. And in so doing we probably make mistakes with our first child that we don't make on those that follow.

The age of the first child also determines where we are in the family life cycle. Several years ago Dr. Evelyn Duvall outlined eight stages of family life.[6] They are:

Stage 1: Married couples (without children).

Stage 2: Childbearing families (oldest child between birth and thirty months).

Stage 3: Families with preschool children (oldest child between two-and-a-half and six years of age).

Stage 4: Families with school children (oldest child between six and thirteen years of age).

Stage 5: Families with teenagers (oldest child between thirteen and twenty years of age).

Stage 6: Families launching young adults (oldest or first child leaves home).

Stage 7: Middle-aged parents (empty nest to retirement).

Stage 8: Aging families (retirement to death of one or both spouses).

As you will note, as the first child matures, the entire family is launched into a new stage of development. The change sometimes requires new or additional skills for successful family living.

This may be why the oldest child is often perceived as an inconvenience or even a threat to some parents. We may sometimes feel uncomfortable with our oldest child because as he or she changes, so must we. About the time we become used to the way our first child functions physically, emotionally, and socially, he changes, through no fault of his own. Simply put, he is growing up.

This point was vividly brought to my attention a few years ago when we were living in Wisconsin. My friend Dr. Frank Bockus and I were traveling to Madison to conduct a seminar on family life. Frank, a successful marriage and family therapist, told me that he and his wife, Alice, had learned something very important about their son, Keith, as he was growing up. About the time they would get used to him at one particular age, say age ten, he would soon become twelve, and frustrations would arise when they tried to treat their twelve-year-old son the way they did when he was ten. And after they accommodated to the world of their twelve-year-old, he soon became fourteen.

Dr. Bockus suggested that some of our problems in families come from parental lag. This is the inability or unwillingness of parents to keep up with or adjust to the development of their children. But if we parents expect to survive the next decade, we must change along with our children.

Of his eldest child, the biblical Jacob said, "Reuben, thou art my firstborn, . . . unstable as water." (Genesis 49:3-4.) This statement may be more revealing of Jacob and Leah than it is of Reuben.

Education for Mothers

The vast majority of the young women in my classes at Brigham Young University are marriage oriented. They want to marry, and most of them will. In addition, they are very committed to having and rearing children of their own.

But young coeds sometimes wonder about combining education, career, marriage, and motherhood. They want it all, but can they have it? And, they constantly ask, should their college education lead toward employment if they plan to marry and have children? They and I have struggled with these concerns, and still do.

Recently I had the opportunity to discuss these issues in more detail with one of my students. She is a mathematics major with a scholarship and is very intelligent and attractive. And she plans to obtain her master's degree. But she asked me a question I could not answer. It was, "Dr. Barlow, do I need a master's degree in math to be a good wife and mother?" She knew I am solidly behind marriage and family life because of the courses I teach. But she also knows I am on record as favoring advanced education or training beyond high school for both young men and young women. So her concern has become mine, and we have not yet resolved it.

One day she brought me two quotations by Brigham Young that have helped her with her dilemma. These thoughts should be of interest to all young LDS women and particularly to those who, like my student, have an interest in mathematics.

Brigham Young stated:

> As I have often told my sisters in the Female Relief societies, we have sisters here who, if they had the privilege of studying, would make just as good mathematicians or accountants as any man; and we think they ought to have the privilege to study these branches of knowledge that they may develop the powers with which they are endowed. We believe that women are useful, not only to sweep houses, wash dishes, make beds, and raise babies, but that they should stand behind the counter, study law or physic [medicine], or become good book-keepers and be able to do the business in any counting house, and all this to enlarge their sphere of usefulness for the benefit of society at large. In following these things they but answer the design of their creation.[7]

On another occasion, Brigham Young noted:

The ladies can learn to keep books as well as the men; we have some few, already, who are just as good accountants as any of our brethren. Why not teach more to keep books and sell goods, and let them do this business, and let the men go to raising sheep, wheat, or cattle, or go and do something or other to beautify the earth and help to make it like the Garden of Eden, instead of spending their time in a lazy, loafing manner?[8]

I believe that education can and should help young women become better wives and mothers. And perhaps as Brigham Young noted, it can also help them develop the powers with which they are endowed and enlarge their sphere of usefulness for the benefit of society. In addition, it may help them answer the design of their creation. But education need not be only in preparation for employment.

I referred to these statements by Brigham Young in one of my columns in the *Deseret News* and received the following letter:

Dear Dr. Barlow:

I was interested in your column in which you discussed a woman enlarging her sphere of usefulness.

Phyllis McGinley wrote a book that is fascinating and that I have enjoyed for years. It is called *Sixpence in Her Shoe* and extols the rewards of homemaking and defends those who prefer to stay at home instead of using their education and experience in the marketplace. I refer you to the chapter entitled "A Jewel in the Pocket." A few quotations from the chapter will tell you how much value an education is to a woman, whether she chooses to have a career outside of the home or to be a full-time homemaker: "Learning is a boon, a personal good. It is a light in the mind, a pleasure for the spirit, an object to be enjoyed. It is refreshment, warmth, illumination, a window from which we get a view of the world. Housewives more than any others deserve well-furnished minds. They have to live in them such a lot of time.

"We who belong to that profession (housewife) hold the fate of the world in our hands. It is our influence that will determine the culture of coming generations. We are the people who chiefly listen to the music, buy the books, attend the theater, prowl the art galleries, collect for the charities, brood over the schools, converse with the children. Our minds need to be rich and flexible for those duties. And even if we had no such duties, we could still honorably wear our education as the ornament it is, with no other excuse than it becomes us. Or if we prefer to keep it in an apron pocket to finger like an amulet, that is also our right. The jewel need not wear out or lose its value or grow dull there, so long as we understand its worth. It is something we have earned by our own efforts. And not even the clamor of household voices or the complaints of a fulminating college dean can destroy for us our job in its possession."

Doesn't she state it well? I have read and reread this book and loved it anew. This book was copyrighted in 1960, but its views never seem to grow old.

Two of my five children are now out of the household, and I have been most grateful for the education I did have in rearing them. I had three years of college before marriage and may finish some day. But a woman can never have too much education. It can only enhance her life if seen in perspective and enjoyed.

When Mothers Work

If LDS wives and mothers do choose to work outside the home, they have serious matters to consider. During the April 1982 general conference, Barbara B. Smith, president of the Relief Society, discussed some of these concerns. Her address, "Her Children Arise Up, and Call Her Blessed," was later printed in the May 1982 *Ensign*.[9] President Smith noted:

The ideal for a family is, and always has been, to have a mother in the home to be with the children, to care for them and to help them grow, to coordinate and correlate the family's activities, and to be a stay against intrusions of unrighteousness. There are times, however, under unusual circumstances, when, in order to help provide for even the basic needs of her family, a mother may be required to accept employment outside her home. As President Ezra Taft Benson has stated, "Many of you often find yourselves in circumstances that are not always ideal . . . who, because of necessity, must work and leave your children with others." . . .

The challenges facing the working mother of small children are many. First, she must find someone to give good care to her child. Next, she has to decide what to do in an emergency situation when there is an accident or sickness. She must rely on the help of an understanding employer, a relative, a neighbor, a schoolteacher, or someone else to help in those times of crisis.

We find that most working mothers organize their time by advance planning, shopping, scheduling, and assigning chores to include each member of the household. They realize the importance of having meals that provide essential nutrients and the warmth of gracious family dining—even though fast food establishments appeal to and even cater to the working-outside-the-home mother as an easier alternative.

We are well aware, however, that the real challenges for many working mothers come in their responsibility for guiding children through periods of questioning and decision making in their times of trouble. These challenges come in being able to sense the unexpressed needs of children and those of which young people, in their immaturity, may not themselves be aware. A mother may not always be on hand when her child's needs seem most acute. But we find that many working mothers take every opportunity to be with their children—to work with them in accomplishing household duties; when it is appropriate, to shop, plan, and play together; and sometimes just to be in the same room so that they have the sense of being with someone who loves them.

It might be a temptation for a working mother to plan special outings and play times as the so-called "quality" time she has with her children. But many are aware of the danger this poses in giving them a distorted picture of life by using all their time together in recreation. It is important for children to see the balance that is necessary between work and play. They need to know that special events are more meaningful when daily routines are established and when assigned duties are completed. . . .

Even though a working mother cannot be the full-time model she might be if she were home with her children, she can help them learn the personal discipline that comes with daily, routine responsibilities, and, afterward, the well-being resulting from praise for work well done.

A woman who must work to care for the needs of her children should learn the essential purposes of life and come to know the Lord and feel his love and direction. Then she can help her children know him and grow to feel secure in our Heavenly Father's love. . . .

Mothers have the special opportunity of bringing children into the world; they can also play a significant role in bringing to pass their success and happiness here as they prepare them for life eternal.

The economic conditions of today present problems to women and their families that have many implications and far-reaching effects. A woman can find solutions as she recognizes the needs that only she can fill and the part that she must play in the Christlike development of her children. As she lives close to the Spirit, that way will be made clear for her. A wife may be compelled to help with the finances of her family. In this matter we have been given direction. President Kimball has stated: "Some women, because of circumstances beyond their control, must work. We understand that. . . . Do not, however, make the mistake of being drawn off into secondary tasks which will cause the neglect of your eternal assignments such as . . . rearing the spirit children of our Father in Heaven. Pray carefully over all your decisions."

5

SEXUALITY

Of all the chapters in this book, this one has created the most interest. After *What Wives Expect of Husbands* was published, one woman called to ask if I planned to write *What Husbands Expect of Wives.* I told her I did, and she replied, "Yes, and I'll bet it will have only one chapter!"

This wife may have exaggerated the point, but she did convey a sentiment common to many women that sex is all a man wants in marriage.

My response was that sexual fulfillment is not the only thing a husband wants, but it is one thing, in fact, one very important thing, that almost all husbands desire in marriage.

But in fairness to husbands, I should add that it is not necessarily the most important. In my survey there were four items with precedence over sexuality. But the item "She helps me attain sexual satisfaction in our relationship" was ranked high by most husbands.

Sexual fulfillment for both husband and wife is no guarantee that other aspects of the marriage will go well. But I do know that when there is little or no sexual fulfillment for either or both spouses, it can affect other dimensions of their relationship.

I was somewhat shocked not long ago at a letter Ann Landers received from a middle-aged woman who said we are preoccupied with sexuality in American marriages. She said she and her husband had given up sexual relationships years ago with no apparent adverse effects on their marriage. She challenged Ann to print the letter to see if others had done the same.

Ann printed the letter and to her amazement received more than 260,000 replies, the greatest number of responses she had ever received to any one article. And what did she find? About half, 130,000, agreed with the woman that sex was over-rated and unnecessary for a fulfilling marriage, and they, too, had given it up.

The other 50 percent (with whom I agree) lamented the fact that so many couples had apparently given up on something that could be so rewarding. Whether or not the 130,000 couples who had given up were representative of a large number of Americans is not known. But one does wonder what percentage of married couples no longer nurture the sexual aspect of marriage.

In my own counseling experience I have found married couples who have little or no sexual interaction because of conflict in their marriages. But others give up their sexual life because they have sought satisfaction with little or no results or they believe that sexual interaction is mostly for reproduction and they have finished having children. Some couples withhold sex as a weapon or bargaining tool.

When Sexual Interests Differ

In their book *A Joyful Meeting: Sexuality in Marriage,*[1] Drs. Mike and Joyce Grace have an interesting chapter on the differences between men and women in sexual matters. During the later years of marriage, it is often the wife who has the stronger sexual interest. But for the first few years of marriage, it is usually the husband. In fact, during the early years of marriage, a young husband is usually interested in sexual interaction about twice as often as his wife.

While the wife's interest in sex can be as intense as that of her husband, it is usually a little more erratic. The husband's interest, however, is intense and more constant. In fact, Drs. Mike and Joyce Grace suggest that a man's interest in sex reoccurs quite regularly, about every forty-eight hours.

If a wife isn't interested in sex but her husband is, should she participate? Before you say no, consider the following.

Most of us grow up with the myth that in order for a sexual encounter to be a good one, the climax or orgasm must be reached simultaneously. This is a myth! If you can achieve it, fine. But 95 percent of a couple's orgasms are achieved independently. Put another way, only 5 percent of orgasms are simultaneous.

Similarly, the probability of two people being simultaneously aroused is quite low. Often one partner will be interested when the other one is not.

I believe few wives realize the capability of sexuality to help keep their husbands close to them physically, emotionally, and even spiritually. When a husband experiences sexual fulfillment he feels very close to his wife in many ways. Because the sexual urge is so strong and constant in men, a wife should realize the high degree of fulfillment that comes to a husband when she helps him attain sexual satisfaction.

On the other hand, I also believe few wives sense the degree of frustration and alienation husbands feel when a wife refuses or ignores his sexual needs and interests. In reality, it is a compliment to her that he finds her sexually desirable. I believe a wise and loving Heavenly Father has given a wife the gift of sexual intimacy to help her achieve oneness with her husband. (See Genesis 2:24-25.)

What if the marital relationship is strained. Should a wife refuse sexual relationships with her husband? If she wants to prolong and heighten the stress, yes. But if she is sincerely interested in improving her relationship with her husband, the answer is a definite no. Dr. Marian Hilliard, an obstetrician, gynecologist, and a woman, gives this advice to her female patients:

> The way to save a strained marriage is to start with the act of love, meaning sexual intercourse. Here are the essentials of marriage in concentrated form. In

one act are consideration, warmth, gaiety, charm, hunger and ecstasy. In this small kingdom, a woman can heal the wounds caused by indifference and contempt. She is a fool, if she ignores this tool provided her by nature. If a woman spent half the time cultivating the sexual relationship with her husband that she sometimes spends avoiding it, her marriage would blossom.[2]

According to Drs. Mike and Joyce Grace, there are at least four ways wives can view sexual intercourse. They are (1) psychological rape, (2) duty or martyrdom, (3) labor of love, and (4) love freely expressed. Let us briefly examine each.

Psychological rape. Some wives may view sex as a form of rape because it is forced on them psychologically rather than physically. In the past, it was considered illegal and sinful for a woman to refuse sex with her husband. And a husband today often may use guilt to force her to participate. He might continually remind her of his unmet sexual needs until she eventually yields to his psychological pressure in order to maintain civility around the house.

But in so doing she usually feels anger and contempt for her husband, and the experience is chalked up as a bad sexual experience. Since she believes she has been sexually violated in marriage, she loses her capacity to enjoy sex. Repeated experiences such as these leave bitter memories that make it extremely difficult for her to have positive feelings about sex, her husband, or herself.

Duty or martyrdom. Sad as it may seem, some wives still believe that sex is a man's prerogative and a woman's duty. The wife who views sexuality as martyrdom usually perceives herself as the good wife who never refuses her husband even though she herself may have little or no interest in sexual endeavors. Both she and the psychologically raped wife see themselves as victims suffering at the hands of another. But the martyr is a heroic victim suffering for a worthwhile cause. For her, sexuality becomes very routine, often perfunctory. There is little fulfillment in sex for her, but she feels rather virtuous about the whole matter.

What martyr wives do not realize is that with her attitude, her husband is not sexually fulfilled either. So both husband and wife end up sexually frustrated. The martyr attitude splits the husband-wife relationship down the middle because it destroys their instinctive feelings of love. Drs. Mike and Joyce Grace note, "Each sexual episode is seen as evidence that the partner doesn't love. This is the exact opposite of what should be taking place. What should be a special way of loving has now become a special curse. Growth is not possible. A cold war is almost inevitable."[3]

Labor of Love. In this category, the woman starts out as the ideal sexual partner, even if it kills her, and emotionally it often does. She tries to force (or fake) erotic response, and, of course, this cannot be done. Again the Graces observe:

> As soon as you start working at sex, erotic feelings go out the window. *Working at sex doesn't work.* So efforts to force a response, instead of narrowing the gap in sexual interest between her and her husband, make it wider instead. Sex becomes a task, and then, a hopeless task. Instead of being fun for her, it is one big headache—a source of feelings of anxiety, inadequacy, guilt and failure. The whole thing has become a nightmare in which erotic feelings will never arise. She will be tempted to slip back into the martyr or psychological-rape situation."[4] (Italics added.)

A wife in this category often gets caught in the trap of trying to make her husband's sexual experiences her own. But, as noted, male and female sexual response can differ. Couples get so caught up in performance and achievement that they forget freedom, affection, humor, playfulness, fun, and love. To enjoy sex, married couples must set themselves free to enjoy sexual intimacy without worrying about how well they perform.

Not long ago I received a letter from a frustrated wife who wrote that she and her husband had sexual relationships frequently, but that she did not enjoy them at all. The main reason, she stated, was that her husband was pressuring her to get excited, to enjoy sex as much as he did. She did, up until the time he started nagging her. The more she tried to enjoy it, the less she did. She enjoyed the closeness but wanted him to relish the excitement.

Must a wife always experience sex exactly as her husband

does? Drs. Mike and Joyce Grace note, "We do not know of any law that says that a woman's pleasure and fulfillment in sexual intercourse has to be measured in orgasms. The fact is that loving and mature women can enjoy sexual intercourse in many different ways."[5]

Love Freely Expressed. Since a woman has the capacity to enjoy sexual intimacy in a variety of ways, she likely will become frustrated if she is forced to duplicate her husband's sexual needs and interests. For sexual fulfillment to occur, a woman should feel free to express her love, tenderness, and creativity in ways that come natural for her. This may mean a full erotic response with orgasms; a partial erotic response without orgasms; and once in a while a response with little or no erotic feeling but that is still deeply sexual, sensitive, and fulfilling. Drs. Mike and Joyce Grace conclude, "Where a woman has this freedom to be herself in making love, and where there is an other-centered love to express, a difference in sexual appetite isn't an insoluble problem. Sexual intercourse can be enjoyed and lived on many levels. Some women even report that they are most deeply moved when the erotic element is absent. The important thing in functioning at "Love Freely Expressed" is freedom and relaxed play with no worries about performance."[6]

The chart on the next page shows the four levels of sexual love more clearly.

Christianity and Sexuality

Many of the letters I receive from my *Deseret News* column pertain to sexuality. One woman wrote:

Dear Dr. Barlow:

My husband and I are deeply committed Christians and have tried to build our marriage and home on Christian ideals.

Our only major problem in marriage is our sexual relationship. For years I have been taught that sex is mostly for reproduction. It has always seemed to be a drudgery to be endured. I don't enjoy it. What is the status of sex in a Christian marriage?

Four Levels of Sexual Love for Wives

Attitudes	Circumstances	Responses	Feelings	Long-Range Effects on Sexual Pleasure
Psychological rape	External compulsion Marriage duty Psychological pressure Marital blackmail	Forced submission	Anger Contempt for husband	Destructive Sex = Violation Sex role bitterness
Duty and/or martyrdom	Sense of obligation Underdeveloped love Lacks knowledge, understanding, and faith in husband	Resigned cooperation	Irritation Feeling that sex is a nuisance Alienation from husband	Destructive Sex – Chore Irksome Resented Sex role resentment
Labor of Love	Determination to be an ideal sexual partner for husband's sake and sake of marriage	Struggle to force an erotic response Pretense	Effort Frustration Dishonesty	Destructive Sex = Problem Sex = Work Sense of inadequacy Sense of failure as a woman
Love Freely Expressed	Sense of Freedom to "be herself" in making love (Impossible to do without husband's acceptance and encouragement)	Spontaneous responses with no preconceived goal	Joy Intimacy Creative fulfillment May or may not be erotic	Constructive Sex = Pleasure Pleased with herself as a woman

Here is my answer:

I have always been impressed with the Reverend Billy Graham. The evangelist addressed this topic in an article entitled "What the Bible Says about Sex."[7] He states, "The Bible celebrates sex and its proper use, presenting it as God-created, God-ordained, God-blessed. It makes plain that God himself implanted the physical magnetism between the sexes for two reasons: For the propagation of the human race, and for the expression of that kind of love between man and wife that makes for true oneness. His command to the first man and woman to be 'one flesh' was as important as his command to 'be faithful and multiply.'"

Graham concludes that "the Bible makes plain that evil, when related to sex, means not the use of something corrupt, but the misuse of something pure and good. It teaches clearly that sex can be a wonderful servant, but a terrible master; that it can be a creative force more powerful than any other in the fostering of love, championship, happiness, or can be the most destructive of all of life's forces.

To the married Christian couples living in Corinth, the apostle Paul admonished:

Because of the temptation to immorality, each man should have his own wife and each woman her own husband.

The husband should give to his wife her conjugal [sexual] rights, and likewise the wife to her husband. For the wife does not rule over her own body, but the husband does; likewise the husband does not rule over his own body, but the wife does.

Do not refuse one another [sexual rights] except perhaps by agreement for a season, that you may devote yourselves to prayer; but then come together again, lest Satan tempt you through lack of self-control. (1 Corinthians 7:2-5, Revised Standard Version.)

This is one of the most positive and mentally healthy statements I have read anywhere regarding sexual relationships. Surely, it has implications for all Christian couples.

While we often view sex as something that makes sinners out of saints, perhaps it could, rightly perceived, help sinners become saints.

The Right to Say No

I received another interesting letter about sexual matters:

Dear Dr. Barlow:

Is a wife supposed to make love with her husband whenever he wants, regardless of how she is feeling about the matter?

Although my husband and I have good sexual experiences together often, this is a constant source of frustration for us. If there are times when I am emotionally not capable of responding sexually, he becomes upset and sulks for days. This, in turn, makes me so upset that I can hardly stand it. Don't I have feelings too? Sometimes I don't even know that I have turned down an invitation until I receive the punishment of silence and sulky behavior.

This was my response:

People should take part in making decisions that affect them as individuals, and this obviously includes the sexual part of marriage. Yes, we do have the right to refuse repeated demands which we deem to be unreasonable.

If you don't feel physically or emotionally capable when the request, or "invitation" as you put it, is made, you could indicate interest but suggest another time you feel might be appropriate.

Perhaps sex is something we share in marriage rather than something we take from or give to each other. And both partners should have an equal opportunity and responsibility in the say-so as to when that should or should not occur. Sex is not a man's prerogative and a woman's duty. That philosophy went out with Model Ts and high button shoes.

After the preceding thoughts were expressed in my column, I again invited written responses. Here is one such letter:

Dear Dr. Barlow:

I like your column but would have given a different answer on the right to say no.

When I was young I was very conscious of my "rights" and of refusing sex if I were not in the mood. But as time went by there were more frustrations, and I found it is hard for both of us to be on a "high" often enough. If a husband is insecure, refusal of sex strikes him as an affront or rejection of him personally. If I were to really extend a firm invitation to my husband and if he were to refuse (which he never does) I might feel hurt. I know how much sex and being loved seem intertwined.

So here is what I do. I know sexual fulfillment makes my husband happy, and I feel good about it too. If I really feel sick or terrible I make sure he knows about it earlier in the day and I make sure he knows it's due to extraneous circumstances. Then he is usually sensitive to me, and I go to bed early. But if he still wants me after all of that, I figure he must need my affection and reassurance, and I do my best to share myself with him. I don't mind in the slightest because I love to please him.

Of course, there are brutish, insensitive husbands, but generally if you put the other person's happiness foremost, you get much of the same back.

Now, I am not always able to do everything in marriage my husband wants. But I am extra sensitive to loving him in sexual ways. And maybe he'll remember me when he is tempted by a younger woman. In other words, I have learned how to be giving and I enjoy it. A wife may make a husband resentful by pushing her "right" to refuse too far. Of course, she has a right. But she must think of what her refusal means to him. And later he may quit asking.

Sexual Stewardship

Rather than viewing sexuality in marriage as something we either give or get, I like to think of it as something a husband and wife can share. It might be called a sexual stewardship.[8]

In the parable of the talents (Matthew 25:14-30), Jesus taught the concept of stewardship, implying that we should improve on whatever has been entrusted to our care. Stewards are managers. And in marriage we are often given joint stewardships, such as children, fidelity, and the day-to-day maintenance of family members, to name a few.

Implied are at least three elements that characterize successful stewardship: (1) agency, (2) diligence, and (3) accountability. We may accept or reject the opportunity to become a steward, but once we accept the responsibility, we are expected to exert great effort, as indicated in the parable of the talents. We are expected to improve or enhance what we have been given. Ultimately there will be an accounting of one kind or another of our various stewardships.

In my marriage seminars at Brigham Young University, we talk about sexuality as a stewardship, including the three concepts of agency, diligence, and accountability. In so doing we read 1 Corinthians 7:2-5 where Paul beautifully describes the sexual stewardship in marriage. I assign each person to write a few comments on the topic "Do We Have a Sexual Stewardship in Marriage?" Following are four excerpts, two from wives and two from husbands, which are representative of the many I have received. One young wife wrote:

> In too many relationships, satisfying personal desires comes first and the partner's needs are secondary. This is contrary to the teaching of Paul. In sexual relations, the role of each partner is, instead, to satisfy the other. They forget about trying to gratify their own desire; each takes care of the other's wants. Having given love unselfishly, both have sexual needs fullfilled in the most rewarding, tender way.
>
> Sometimes we worry that if we don't look after ourselves, no one will—we might never get what we want unless we take it. This philosophy has no place in the teachings of Christ.

Another wife wrote:

> To be a steward means that a person is given the responsibility to nourish, protect, and care for something. Therefore, to have a sexual stewardship would mean that a person has the responsibility of nourishing, protecting, and caring for the sexual part of his or her marriage. This must be a joint stewardship between the husband and wife.
>
> Just as a person doesn't want any harm to come to any of his possessions, he would not want any harm to come to his spouse, because he is her steward. It is suggested that the body of the one is for the pleasure of the other and that this pleasure should not be withheld because it is the right of the other. The steward is responsible to see that this is done with deep concern and love so that both will be able to fulfill their stewardships while sharing their love.
>
> Another aspect of stewardships is that there is always a time of accounting. I believe that this too will be a part of our sexual stewardship. Each of us will be held accountable for how we treated our spouses and whether we were truly unselfish in giving our love.

A husband in my class gave this description of sexual stewardship:

> In discussing this part of marriage, my wife and I have both come to strongly believe that a sexual stewardship is vital to our relationship. For us, the most important part of the stewardship is the sharing, or in other words, a joint stewardship. Like all aspects of our marriage, if we are not both trying to satisfy and make the other happy, then not much can come from anything we do.
>
> We have talked about the differences we have in our sexual needs, but we do not think that this means that one has to have more responsibility for stew-

ardship than the other. For example, my wife tends to be more romantic than I am. Therefore, I have a stewardship or responsibility to see that I treat her as affectionately as possible, and make it a priority to spend romantic or intimate time with her. If I do not, I have not fulfilled my share of the stewardship. I tend to be quite a bit more pragmatic than my wife, and she has the stewardship to be sensitive to those feelings and understand when I may not be too romantic.

When we are both considerate of each other's needs, feelings are seldom hurt and we both find satisfaction in the relationship.

Part of stewardship may include doing things for your spouse when you do not feel like it, but in our sexual relationship we view this somewhat differently. We both believe that there must be a mutual interest or desire in order to achieve satisfaction in intimate or sexual relations. It somehow just does not seem right to us if this is not so. We feel that it is as much a part of our stewardship to be patient and understanding as it is to satisfy each other's intimate desires.

Another young husband wrote:

A sexual stewardship is a couple stewardship, not an individual one. Many people have the false notion that the sexual stewardship is the man's responsibility because, after all, "men are the ones interested in sex." Men and women were not created unequal in sexual response or desire. The husband's sex drive isn't any more intense or important than the wife's; it is only more constant.

In our marriage we both recognize that sexual desires are holy and a gift to us from God to use to draw closer together and to people the earth. We are trying to practice the principles found in 1 Corinthians 7:2-5. We never use sex as a punishment by withholding it from each other when we are angry or upset. Another interesting concept we have learned is that our bodies are for the fulfillment of each other. This has brought a "giving" instead of "taking" attitude in our sexual life.

A Marital Myth

During the past few years Latter-day Saint counselors have been giving greater attention to sexuality in marriage. The October 1981 convention of the Association of Mormon Counselors and Psychotherapists (AMCAP), held in Salt Lake City, included many discussions on sexuality.

Two participants at the conference, Dr. Corydon Hammond and Dr. Robert Stahmann, presented a paper on "Sex Therapy with LDS Couples."[9] They noted:

A widespread myth exists in the LDS culture. The myth is that sexual problems are only a manifestation of marital discord and conflict. Therefore, if the relationship is enhanced, the sexual dysfunction will automatically resolve itself. . . .

It is . . . true that some sexual problems originate from marital discord. Many couples seeking sexual therapy also need marital therapy, which we employ prior to focusing on the sexual dysfunctions. However, in most instances, sexual dysfunctions will not resolve themselves even if the marriage relationship improves.

Drs. Hammond and Stahmann cited several studies that document that happily married couples can have sexual dysfunctions. One such study, reported in the *New England Journal of Medicine*, indicated that 83 percent of some couples not in therapy reported their marriages "happy" or "very happy." Yet, despite the high degree of marital happiness, 63 percent of the women and 40 percent of the men reported a sexual dysfunction.

The authors suggested that sexual dysfunction does not have to cause disruption of the entire marital relationship. They concluded:

Where there is emotional intimacy and high satisfaction in other areas of the marriage, some couples are successful in tolerating sexual problems with minimal disruption by compartmentalizing and insulating them from the rest of the relationship. However, sexual intimacy and fulfillment are important and valued by most couples, and sexual dysfunction can, over a period of time, frequently cause deep resentment, emotional distance, and deterioration in the marriage.

Latter-day Saint couples ought not, therefore, assume that because a sexual problem exists that something is terribly wrong with their marriage. Many sexual dysfunctions, like other marital problems, can be dealt with adequately by the couple with patience, perseverance, knowledge, skills, and motivation. On occasion, however, couples may need outside professional help.

The Sexually Well Person

At the same AMCAP convention, Dr. Val MacMurray gave an interesting profile of what he believed to be a sexually well person.[10] (In the profile Dr. MacMurray used the feminine pronouns her and she, but noted that the concepts apply to men as well as women.) He stated:

> I think to the extent that the sexually well person accepts and appreciates her sexuality, it would become a force that made her relationship with herself, with her spouse, and with her God better, stronger, and more binding. In other words, sexuality would not be an unacknowledged element in a person's life, something she tried to ignore about herself, something that was present but not talked about in the marriage relationship, or a part of one's life from which God was excluded. It would be prayed over and for. In fact, I am convinced that the dominant attitude of the sexually well person toward her sexuality would be gratitude. . . .
>
> 1. The sexually well person would feel gratitude towards her own body for its ability to respond to pleasure. . . . Someone who is grateful for her body will respect and appreciate it. She does not deny it, or ignore it. On the contrary, she pays proper attention to it, and welcomes appropriate opportunities to understand its possibilities and potentialities.
>
> 2. The sexually well person would feel gratitude to her husband. The possibility of loving a well-beloved other should be a tremendous source of happiness, especially since it is mingled with the realization that our own fulfillment has been made possible by that same spouse's desire to give pleasure as well as receive it. Related to this, and I think it is fairly obvious, there is a sense of unique bonding created by that sexual union. We break bread with many people. We even share our hopes and fears with many people, though certainly not to equal degrees. Though the idea is losing popularity in the culture and society around us, one of the characteristics of a healthy marriage is its sexual fidelity—the luxuriant certainty that only the two of you know and understand that part of the relationship, that only the two of you share that activity, that pleasure, that learning and loving.
>
> 3. The sexually well person would also feel grateful to God, not only for the blessing of a physical body, but for knowing and loving another person, and, in a temple marriage, for the sealing ordinances that make the possibility of that union extend beyond death. In addition, just as sexual activity can enhance our respect and love for our own bodies and can increase our loving knowledge of our spouses, so our sexual activity can increase our love, reverence and knowledge of our heavenly parents. Obviously much of our mortal probation is designed to help us develop godly attributes by giving us opportunities for growth. . . . Such opportunity to understand godliness occurs in the cherished privacy of our most intimate relationships as husbands and wives. . . .

If our chief attitudes toward our sexuality were respect, appreciation, and gratitude instead of fear, guilt, or perhaps anger, what would we teach ourselves, and our children? How would we reteach concepts that may have been badly learned in the first place. And how would we go about healing some of the wounds left by damaging experiences that people have had up to this point?

I suspect that we would want to emphasize the holiness of sexuality and eliminate some of the mysteriousness which makes it frightening and tempting. It would not be something that separates us from God, but something that links us to him.

6

Communication

The Family Service Association of America once made a careful four-year study of American families to see why marriages fail. The findings included the usual things we blame, such as conflicts over money, children, sex, leisure, relatives, and infidelity. One or more of these occurred in about 35 percent of all the troubled couples studied. Other difficulties, such as housekeeping conflicts and physical abuse, were listed on an average of 16 percent of the time. Difficulties with communication, however, were listed far and above anything else as a major factor in marital disruption. It was reported that 86 percent of those who experienced marital failure indicated they had communication problems. The surveys reported time and time again that husbands and wives had a common complaint: "We can't talk to each other."[1]

In my own surveys one of the noticeable differences was that wives ranked communication very high in importance, number one in most instances. Husbands, on the other hand, did not rank communication quite as high as did wives. In fact, in my survey they ranked it only sixth. Dr. Joyce Brothers noted in her book *What Every Woman Should Know about Men* that men, in general, tend to talk about themselves less than women. This suggests that husbands tend to be less personal in their conversations with their wives.

Husbands Comment

Even though communication was not ranked as high by men as by women, husbands did perceive communication to be an important part of marriage. One husband commented:

> One of the great problems in marriage today is the lack of communication between husbands and wives. My brother is on the edge of divorce and is married to a wife who will not listen to him or even talk very much. She is unaware that she is quick-tempered and appears to many to be self-centered. When my brother tries to bring these things up, she just walks away from him.

Still another husband believes the ability to communicate is directly related to sexual satisfaction in marriage. He wrote:

> I think most people quietly hide behind failure in sexual compatibility because they feel they cannot communicate with their marriage partner or seek assistance from others. Discussing such intimate relationships requires a great deal of confidence in someone else.
>
> There is, however, one key to successful sexual compatibility between married couples. You cannot solve that as a problem when there are other problems in the marriage. For that matter, you cannot really solve it as a problem until you are doing well in the other areas of your relationship. This would include communicating in a nonthreatening way.
>
> I found that our best problem-solving discussions take place when we are communicating well in all the other areas of married life. Then, when we turn to the issues of intimate relations, we are more open and honest about our feelings.

Listening

As was noted in chapter 3, a husband needs a confidante, someone to whom he can confide his deepest feelings. When I have suggested this to wives in my marriage seminars, many are shocked. They state that they have tried for years to get a husband to "open up" with little or no success. But one complaint many husbands have is that wives talk too much and do not listen enough.

While it is generally acknowledged that in communication there must be both a sender and a receiver, we have all too often focused first and sometimes only on the sending aspect. The tragic truth is that many do not care to listen to others. They want to be understood but really do not care to understand.

In his book *Helping Couples Change,* Dr. Richard Stuart says, "For golden words to be of value, the sender and receiver are required to be equally proficient in totally different procedures and skills. Without the ability to listen, we would be doomed to a life of monologue rather than dialogue, and we would be locked into a closed information system that would make adaptation to changing living conditions all but impossible. Despite its great significance, most people take listening for granted until it breaks down entirely, much as they take for granted, until times of crisis, their breathing and heartbeat."[2]

S. I. Hayakawa, the well-known semanticist, once noted that listening, for most people, is "simply maintaining a polite silence while you are rehearsing in your mind the speech you are going to make the next time you can grab a conversational opening." We should not belittle the ability to keep quiet, in thought as well as voice, while another is speaking. I have always maintained that the Holy Ghost tells a person both when to speak up and when to shut up. When trying to communicate, perhaps we need greater inspiration in the latter than we do the former.

But silence in and of itself does not mean, as Hayakawa notes, that a person is actually listening or interested in what another has to say. While we are quiet we may be rejecting the other's words because they appear to be boring, simplistic, or complicated. Or, we may pay more attention to the sender's appearance and mannerisms than we do his words. We can, in addition, place too much emphasis on a single word or sentence. And all along, as Hayakawa suggests, we may be preparing our next speech, regardless of what the other person is saying.

What, then, are characteristics of good listeners? Dr. Richard Stuart suggests there are at least four components:

1. Good listeners are fully committed to listen.
2. Good listeners are physically and mentally ready to listen.

3. Good listeners wait for the other to complete a message before attempting to express their own ideas.

4. Good listeners use analytic skills to supplement, not replace, listening.[3]

Commitment to listen (1) involves deciding that the words of a husband or wife are important enough to hear. This needs to be decided long before the actual conversation begins. The willingness to listen may be physically or mentally indicated (2) by relaxing, turning off the television, putting down the newspaper, sitting erect and maintaining appropriate eye contact. Waiting one's turn to speak (3) involves not jumping in to complete the other's sentence, not asking for more information before the other has completed an expression, and providing nonverbal signs of interest in what is being said. Being able to repeat and accurately rephrase the other's message is a good example of number 4, the proper use of analytic communication skills to supplement listening.

By using the above and other appropriate listening skills, wives would be in a better position to be the willing listeners that most husbands want. Wives should also remember that many extramarital affairs begin with a woman who is willing to genuinely listen to another woman's husband. Wives who are poor listeners influence husbands to seek satisfaction of this need elsewhere.

Communication Skills from the Scriptures

Sometimes contemporary marriage counselors think they are the ones who originated the concept that people ought to communicate effectively with each other. And it is true that they have made great progress in this area. But people have had concerns about effective communication for thousands of years.

Solomon was such a person. Solomon, you will remember, had seven hundred wives and likely would have become very knowledgeable about communication.

What suggestions did King Solomon have for wives and others about effective communication? In the book of Proverbs,

Solomon gives the following suggestions. The scriptures are listed in ten groups with a central theme for each. Can you decide what the theme is for each of the ten groups?

1. Proverbs 11:9; 12:18; 15:4; 18:8, 21; 26:22. (See also James 3:2-10; 1 Peter 3:10.)
2. Proverbs 4:20-23; 6:12, 14, 18; 16:2, 23.
3. Proverbs 15:31; 18:13, 15; 19:20; 21:28. (See also James 1:19.)
4. Proverbs 12:18; 14:29; 15:28; 16:32; 21:23; 26:4; 29:20.
5. Proverbs 15:23; 25:11.
6. Proverbs 10:19; 11:12-13; 13:3; 17:27-28; 18:2; 20:19; 21:23.
7. Proverbs 17:9; 21:9.
8. Proverbs 15:1, 4; 16:1; 25:15.
9. Proverbs 12:16; 19:11.
10. Proverbs 12:17, 22; 16:13; 19:5; 26:18-19, 22; 28:23; 29:5. (See also Ephesians 4:25; Colossians 3:9.)

Measured Openness and Honesty in Communication

Recently one of my students asked in a marriage class if it was best to be totally open and honest in marriage. I asked him and the other class members what they thought, and they all agreed that husbands and wives should be totally open and honest in their marital communication. I told the class I agreed if "being totally open and honest" meant we should not blatantly lie, cheat, or do anything that would be deceitful or cause mistrust.

But, I suggested, there is another dimension that needs consideration. Does being totally open and honest mean I should say everything and anything on my mind? Should I always express exactly how I feel?

A few years ago many, including the experts, would have said, "Yes, let it all hang out." Today, there is some question about this philosophy. Rather than "letting it all hang out," many are advocating *measured* openness and honesty in marital communication.

I explained to my class that day what measured openness and honesty meant. I asked each of them to think of one of their very best friends of the same sex. I suggested they recall for a moment some of the past experiences they had had with that valued friend. Did they appreciate having such a friend? What did they do to protect and enhance their friendship?

I asked if they expressed every little petty concern that arose between them and their friend. While not suggesting that such concerns always be concealed, I asked when and under what circumstances should a concern or even a criticism be raised? We agreed that we usually disclose such things only when they are necessary to sustain and strengthen the friendship.

We then compared the husband-wife relationship to friendship. What would we say, or not say, to protect the relationship? Would we air every minor concern or would some things just best be left unsaid? Would the tone of voice and the timing be important? Would we make sure we showed "an increase of love" (D&C 121:43) after a confrontation to make sure the relationship was maintained?

Recent research has suggested that vented hostility usually generates more hostility and that repeated gripes do little to reduce the frequency or intensity of undesirable behavior. If, however, we carefully control what we say, the relationship will likely prosper.

The question logically arises as to when to convey a concern or when to just tolerate it. I believe that if a problem continues for a long time and disrupts daily routines such as sleeping, eating and working, it should be discussed and hopefully resolved. This is particularly true if the problem is becoming more and more serious.

On the other hand, many of our concerns can be dealt with by increasing our level of tolerance rather than constantly demanding or expecting a marriage partner to change to meet our expectations. Before discussing such concerns, ask yourself: Will discussing this concern improve our relationship? Will we become better friends by so doing? If the answer is no, the problem is probably better left unmentioned. Morris L. Ernst once noted, "A sound marriage is not based on complete frankness. It is based on a sensible reticence."

Setting the Stage

A few months ago I was invited to be on a television talk show to discuss my book *What Wives Expect of Husbands*. I arrived a little early and watched the stage crew set the stage for the brief interview that was to follow. The lights were meticulously adjusted and the chairs and microphone precisely placed. Finally we went on the air. I thought to myself afterward that a lot of work went into setting the stage for just a few minutes of conversation. But setting the stage does make a difference in communication whether on television or in our everyday lives.

Many students at Brigham Young University have come to talk to me about marriage. Often they will have something important to say to a spouse and want to discuss with me how to do it. Usually, they want to discuss the *content* of their message.

But before discussing content, I like to discuss *process* with my students. For instance, I like to discuss the *where* and the *when* of communication as well as the *how* and the *what*. In essence, we set the stage for effective communication. And usually we talk about *timing* and *privacy*.

Timing. It should be obvious to most couples that certain times are more appropriate than others to discuss important matters. I have found in my own marriage that five minutes before our evening meal is not the most opportune time to discuss my deepest, most sensitive feelings. Susan simply has other things on her mind at that time. And she has found out by now that trying to talk to me about important issues while I am trying to figure out income taxes is somewhat less than futile.

Times of fatigue, hunger, illness, sickness, exams, or other stress are not the best times to discuss important matters. Susan and I have found that some of our best talks have occurred at two or three o'clock in the morning when children are asleep. It is very quiet. And after a few hours of sleep we are rested to the point that we can talk rationally and calmly. Besides, there are no telephone calls, knocks on the door, or any other distractions. It is important to find a time to communicate without interruptions and distractions.

Privacy. On occasion, Susan and I will go to one of our favorite restaurants to discuss an important concern. This is particularly true if we cannot find privacy at home. Not only is the atmosphere of a favorite restaurant conducive to an open exchange of ideas, but a good meal tends to mellow me and, to some degree, Susan as well.

When my students have something important to discuss with a fiance or spouse, I suggest they drive up the canyon, go to a park, go for a walk, or go anywhere to get away from interruptions and distractions for a few hours. Both timing and privacy seem to be important parts of setting the stage for good communication.

Silence, Consistency, and Respect

In their book *A Guide to Successful Marriage,*[4] Albert Ellis and Robert Harper have some suggestions to improve communication between husbands and wives. Here are three of their ideas:

Silence. Someone once noted that "silence is golden," but prolonged silence lasting hours, days, or even weeks tends to be detrimental to marital relationships. Mahatma Gandhi used silence as a means of protest against his enemies, not his loved ones. And I have always maintained that prolonged silence is a high form of communication—it means we can't or won't talk! During times of stress or conflict, a husband and wife should continue to talk about less emotionally charged issues to bridge the emotional gap that comes during the silent treatment. "Please pass the butter" or "Did you pick up the clothes from the cleaners" should not be threatening words. Yet the inability or unwillingness to say even such routine things usually disrupts a marriage.

Consistency. According to Ellis and Harper, communication

in marriage often breaks down because husbands and wives believe that everything they and their spouse will do will be logical, consistent, and rational. The fact is, a great deal of what we say, do, and think is often illogical, inconsistent, and irrational.

Why, for instance, will Susan drive our large station wagon several extra miles to a distant grocery store to save three cents on a can of tuna? For the same reason that I will drive the same number of miles to save two cents on a gallon of gas, of course.

Why must the furniture in our house be routinely rearranged or the butter kept on the refrigerator shelf rather than in the cupboard? How can I justify a fishing trip that costs nearly one hundred dollars and come home with a seven-inch trout when trout are on sale at the supermarket?

Harper and Ellis remind us that husbands and wives are not always logical, rational, or consistent, and the degree to which we expect them to be so disrupts communication. They note, "Logic has little, if anything, to do with some of the habits that people develop. Many communication difficulties in marriage can be removed or reduced by helping people to stop looking for logic as the basis for the life-long habits of themselves and their mates."[5]

Respect as a Person. Most husbands and wives try to communicate with each other in some role he or she is performing. We do not often think of a spouse as a person but as someone who does something—mate, partner, breadwinner, or housekeeper. Harper and Ellis suggest that when spouses are elevated to the status of a respected friend, marital relationships vastly improve. They note, "It is . . . not our words that matter nor the principle of this or that thing, nor what others think of us. . . . The one and paramount thing which really matters is the personality of the mates themselves. Their individual likes and dislikes, preferences and distastes, ideas and attitudes. If each partner in the marriage learns to deal respectfully and lovingly with the you, me, and us of the relationship, meanings will be enjoyable much of the time."[6]

Patterns of Communication

Dr. Virginia Satir is a well-known marriage counselor and

therapist who has written an informative book entitled *Peoplemaking*. Dr. Satir has conceptualized faulty communication into four distinct patterns: distracting, computing, blaming, and placating.

The *distractor* often says things that are irrelevant to the conversation and never makes a simple, straightforward response. He or she may ignore what is being said by failing to reply, walking away, changing the subject, or turning to talk to someone else. Distractors often win arguments by simply shifting to a new topic during the exchange or conversation.

The *computer* is very reasonable, logical, and rational. His or her emotions are completely in control, and the computer's voice is usually a dry monotone lacking animation. Convictions are often expressed in abstract terms with detailed analysis of the situation. Computers usually feel that it is very important to say the right words and to show little or no feelings. He or she often ignores the feelings of the other and does not listen to the meaning behind the words. Discussions are usually reduced to an abstract analysis of words, phrases, or sentences.

The *blamer* acts like a dictator, boss, or fault-finder. His or her voice is often tight, shrill, or loud. The blamer not only fails to listen but often spends a great deal of time and energy riding roughshod over the other person and his or her feelings. The motto of a blamer is, "The best defense is attack."

The *placater* is just the opposite of the blamer. He or she tries to please or apologize and never disagrees, no matter how great the provocation. The voice of a placater is often whiny or squeaky. Placaters usually say yes to everything despite their true thoughts and feelings. They seldom achieve anything they want, so there is little possibility of genuine satisfaction through mutual interaction. Failure to achieve such mutual interaction usually lowers the self-esteem of both partners.

Dr. Satir recommends a fifth method of communicating that is open, honest, and direct. It tries to increase, rather than decrease, the self-esteem of those involved. This method is called *leveling*. Leveling conveys as precisely as possible what a person thinks or feels with no attempt to placate, blame, compute, or distract. A leveler's verbal response is consistent with his or her body language, gestures, and facial expressions. If a leveler says, "I love you," the voice and gesture are warm. If he says, "I am angry with you," both verbal and nonverbal messages are straightforward, unambiguous, and clear.

According to Dr. Satir, leveling is the only kind of communication that makes it possible to live in harmony and mutual self-enhancement in marriage. Leveling heals ruptures, breaks impasses, and builds bridges between the couple. A person who levels allows himself to live as a whole person, in touch with his head, heart, feelings, and body. Dr. Satir notes, "Being a leveler enables you to have integrity, commitment, honesty, intimacy, competence, creativity, and the ability to work with real problems in a real way. The other forms of communication (distracting, computing, blaming, and placating) result in doubtful integrity, . . . dishonesty, loneliness, and shoddy competence."[7]

When a married couple learns to appropriately level with each other, they are able to function from a firm base of self-esteem, optimism, and feelings of integrity. This maximizes their chances for contentment, satisfaction, and success in marriage, and for their happiness in other relationships as well.

Feelings and Expectations

Much of what we call communication is actually a simple relaying of information, much like the information given by television newscasters. Usually the information is pertinent, informative, accurate, and necessary. Examples of such information are, "Sally got an A in Algebra"; "Bob got a new job"; "It looks like it is going to storm today"; and "Do you know what is wrong with the vacuum?" We do need to exchange this kind of information. But to deeply understand and be understood, we need eventually to get to feelings and expectations.

Feelings. During the course of each day most of us will ask or be asked more than once, "How are you today?" While this is sometimes a genuine concern of another, we customarily do not give a serious reply. Dr. David Mace, marriage counselor and educator, has noted:

> The process of being socialized includes careful training on how to conceal our true inner feelings. Unfortunately, this is poor training for married life. A perceptive psychiatrist once observed that there is little or nothing in our culture that prepares us for the honest accounting that is essential for success in intimate relationships. So, having learned to wear masks all day outside the home, many married couples habitually conceal their real selves from each other, and in consequence never achieve the closeness and trust that are essential for true intimacy.[8]

So, "How are you feeling?" is a question of paramount importance in marriage. In fact, the quality of the relationship may well be measured by the degree of honesty with which this question is answered. In addition, the degree of caring and compassion with which the response is accepted is also vital.

Dr. Mace suggests a simple exercise to help married couples discuss their feelings. Sit down together with a paper and pencil, and, separately, write down a list of all your present feelings. Most people can easily recognize eight or ten feelings at any given time. Many are surprised at this.

After ten minutes of writing, share with each other the list you have made. Then talk about your lists. What feelings are you reluctant to share with each other? Which are embarrassing to you? Which represent barriers to mutual understanding? This is a good way to more fully understand each other's feelings.

Expectations. All of us come into marriage with a wide array of expectations from a variety of sources. We have expectations of our marriage, our marriage partner, and ourselves. Some of our expectations may be excessive or even unrealistic, but we have them, just the same.

How many times have you caught yourself saying or thinking "I wish my wife or husband would . . ."? Or, have you ever asked yourself during your marriage "I wonder if he or she wants me to . . . ?" Dr. Carlfred Broderick, noted marriage counselor from the University of Southern California, has recently observed, "We can continue for years doing things (or failing to do things) without realizing that they are hurtful to our partners. Often, however, small changes in our behavior—changes that actually cost us very little—can mean a great deal to our marriage partner."[9]

Dr. Broderick suggests that rather than just wishing and wondering our life away regarding our marital expectations, we can use what he calls "wish lists."

The first step in using a wish list is for both husband and wife to make a short list of wished-for changes in their spouse's behavior. Both partners should write down three or four specific changes that a spouse could accomplish during the next seven days. The expectations must be positive, specific, "small," and done frequently, and they should not be focused on areas of sharp conflict. By learning to meet small expectations, we gain skills and insights to help us meet the larger, more sensitive ones later.

A positive request requires an increase in desired behaviors, not a decrease in unwanted behaviors. "Please ask me how I spent my day" is a positive request that is better understood and received than a negative request such as "Don't ignore me so much." A specific request is one such as "Come home at six o'clock for dinner" rather than the vague "Show more consideration for me and the family." A smaller, more manageable request such as "Help the children keep their bicycles in the proper place in the garage" is much clearer and more easily accomplished than "Do a better job in training the children."

After both wish lists are written and understood, the couple should proceed to the next step, negotiation. In the negotiating phase, a husband and wife simply agree on what they can or will do on each other's list. One partner may be willing to work on just one or two of the other's wishes if he or she will be willing to do just one in return. The negotiating should be done in a playful, competitive, and zestful manner. And the husband and wife may want to do some bargaining. One husband agreed to do everything on his wife's wish list if she would agree to try to accomplish the first item on his. Both were equally happy with the arrangement.

Husbands and wives may also negotiate penalties if either violates their original agreement. Such penalties should be minor and even fun. One wife agreed to bake her husband's favorite pie if she did not follow through. He agreed to buy her a new sweater if he failed to live up to what he said he would do.

After seven days, the wish lists can be continued, renegotiated, or discontinued.

A Concluding Thought

Most husbands and wives do not think of communication as an active, involved process. Most merely think of it as something "we just do." By giving more thought and attention to what they say, or don't say, most couples would likely find their relationship improved. Good communication is based upon attitudes and skills that are consciously learned and practiced over a period of time, much as a couple would construct a bridge. An anonymous poet has left us the following to consider:

Precaution

They say a wife and husband, bit by bit
Can rear between their lives a mighty wall
So thick they cannot speak with ease through it,
Nor can they see across, it stands so tall.
Its nearness frightens them, but each alone
Is powerless to tear its bulk away;
And each, heartbroken, wishes he had known
For such a wall the magic word to say.

So let us build with master art, my dear,
A bridge of faith between your life and mine—
A bridge of tenderness and very near—
A bridge of understanding, strong and fine;
Till we have built so many lovely ties,
There never will be room for walls to rise.[10]

7

SELF-ESTEEM

It probably is not surprising to many women that most husbands want a wife who thinks well of herself and exhibits a certain amount of confidence and self-acceptance. We simply might say that husbands want a wife with high self-esteem. And yet, this may be easier stated than achieved. A recent poll indicated that 37 percent of Americans have high self-esteem, 33 percent have average self-esteem, and 30 percent have low self-esteem. Also of interest was the fact that those with feelings of low self-worth reported more symptoms of stress and poor health.[1]

The importance of self-esteem for both husbands and wives was also illustrated in a letter I recently received. It read:

Dear Dr. Barlow:

Our marriage has not been ideal. Many times commitment was the only thing that kept us together. I really think that our most crippling problem through all the years of our marriage has been lack of self-esteem with both my husband and myself. And we have apparently passed low esteem on to our children.

Lately we began to read about the importance of self-esteem and during the past year took a community education course on the topic.

Realizing that low self-esteem was at the base of most of our problems, the things we learned proved to be very helpful to us. We were both raised in families where duty and performance were more important than being valued as a person. And we now have a difficult time doing things just for pure enjoyment without feeling guilty.

The more I like myself, the more I love my husband and can accept his weaknesses. I just wish I had learned this earlier in our marriage.

When self-esteem is low, not only does the person suffer, as indicated in the letter, but those around him or her usually suffer as well. Elder Neal A. Maxwell probably summed it up best in ten simple words: "If I am not happy with me, other people suffer."[2] And when wives and mothers are unhappy with themselves, it usually means that their husbands and children will experience the consequences right along with them.

Because of the mother's monumental influence on the home and family, she is the one who can least afford to suffer from low self-esteem. Her influence on her husband and children has not only mortal but eternal consequences.

If low esteem turns to hostility, things become even worse. Albert Ellis, noted psychologist, has observed, "We get angry with others in direct proportion that we are angry with ourselves."[3] This statement may give some insight as to why so many husbands and wives get so easily irritated with others so frequently. In reality, they may be angry at themselves, venting and directing the hostility toward other family members.

Self-Esteem and Communication

It is more than just coincidence that this chapter on self-esteem follows the one on communication. In his book *The Individual, Marriage, and the Family,* Lloyd Saxton notes that effective communication is closely related to self-esteem: "Communication that is disruptive, belittling, or argumentative tends to lower the self-esteem of the other person, whereas communication that is open, honest, clear, and nondefensive tends to enhance the self-esteem of others."[4]

Enhancing self-esteem, therefore, is a key factor in achieving marital satisfaction and interaction.

Saxton further comments:

A person who has positive feelings of self-esteem is characterized by integrity, responsibility, and the ability to express affection and love. Acting from a firm base of appreciating his or her own worth, such a person is able to appreciate the worth of others. A person characterized by positive feelings of self-esteem attacks problems realistically, thus maximizing the possibility for resolving them. This leads to a relatively great number of success experiences, so that the person with high self-esteem is characteristically optimistic and cheerful, expecting things to go well. When things do not go well, the problems are assumed to be temporary difficulties that will yield to sustained effort. Maintaining a high level of self-esteem is facilitated by receiving recognition and praise from others whose opinions we respect.

In contrast with a person who has high self-esteem, someone who characteristically feels a relatively low level of self-esteem is not surprised by persistent failure and, indeed, may expect it. Each failure confirms this expectation. The person with low self-esteem who anticipates failure rarely puts forth his or her best efforts, but erects protective walls of isolation and distrust that provide protection from expected slights, depreciation, and attacks—withdrawing into apathy and loneliness.[5]

A Declaration of Self-Esteem

In her book *Peoplemaking,* Dr. Virginia Satir talks about the importance of self-esteem and notes that if we don't have it, we can get it. The most important message in her book is that one's life can change because he can always learn new things. She states that people can and do change because they are living beings. As we grow older, change may take longer, but it can and does occur, just the same. Satir observes, "Knowing that change is possible, and wanting to do it, are two first big steps. We may be slow learners, but we are all educable."[6] Dr. Satir then concludes with what she calls "My Declaration of Self-Esteem":

I am me.

In all the world, there is no one else exactly like me. There are persons who have some parts like me, but no one adds up exactly like me. Therefore, everything that comes out of me is authentically mine because I alone chose it.

I own everything about me—my body, including everything it does; my mind, including all its thoughts and ideas; my eyes, including the images of all they behold; my feelings, whatever they may be—anger, joy, frustration, love, disappointment, excitement; my mouth, and all the words that come out of it, polite, sweet, or rough, correct or incorrect; my voice, loud or soft; and all my actions, whether they be to others or to myself.

I own my fantasies, my dreams, my hopes, my fears.

I own all my triumphs and successes, all my failures and mistakes.

Because I own all of me, I can become intimately acquainted with me. By so doing I can love me and be friendly with me in all my parts. I can then make it possible for all of me to work in my best interests.

I know there are aspects about myself that puzzle me, and other aspects that I do not know. But as long as I am friendly and loving to myself, I can courageously and hopefully look for the solutions to the puzzle and for ways to find out more about me.

However I look and sound, whatever I say and do, and whatever I think and feel at a given moment in time is me. This is authentic and represents where I am at that moment in time.

When I review later how I looked and sounded, what I said and did, and how I thought and felt, some parts may turn out to be unfitting. I can discard that which is unfitting, and keep that which proved fitting, and invent something new for that which I discarded.

I can see, hear, feel, think, say, and do. I have the tools to survive, to be close to others, to be productive, and to make sense and order out of the world of people and things outside of me.

I own me, and therefore I can engineer me.

I am me and I am okay.[7]

Eleven Ways to Build Self-Esteem

Dr. Robert H. Schuller, religious leader and lecturer, has also commented on the importance of high self-esteem.[8] He notes:

It would be hard for me to overstress the importance of self-esteem. As strong and happy self-esteem grows, our work gets better, our personal relationships improve, we feel more cheerful, healthier—everything takes on a new and friendlier face.

The person with self-esteem develops and expresses a very healthy self-confidence. Lack of self-confidence is one of the major roadblocks to peace of mind, happiness and success in life. Self-confidence is your belief in your own ability to come to grips with problems and solve them; to know that you can and will succeed at worthy tasks. Self-confidence equips you emotionally to meet life's challenges with equanimity and self-reliance.

The self-confident person, in turn, dares to be honest and open. He accepts himself as a unique individual. He reflects a basic integrity of character. He becomes genuinely and infectiously enthusiastic.

Here are eleven ways, according to Dr. Schuller, to improve self-esteem:

1. *Handle Your Competition Creatively:* Competition, like water, left to the uncontrolled floods of [negative] thinking, can drown one's self-esteem. But controlled, . . . competition becomes one of our most dynamic and constructive forces. Focus on yourself, not on others. Compete against yourself and you cannot lose!

2. *Be Your Own Best Booster:* Start being your own best booster by listening seriously to your own bright and big ideas. Give your dreams a boost and you will surprise yourself by making your wonderful, impossible ideas turn a corner and become a possibility.

3. *Develop a Plan for Dealing with Your Own Imperfections:* We all have them. When you learn to accept and deal constructively with your imperfections, you will make enormous strides in the all-important business of building mature and secure self-esteem.

4. *Forgive Yourself:* Learn to forgive yourself for mistakes you may have made in the past, even if the past is as recent as yesterday. Every day is a new beginning. . . . Instead of being tempted to nurse regrets with the destructive phrase "I wish I had," you will look to the future and say, "Next time I will."

5. *Accept What Cannot Be Changed:* Don't resent the shape of your face or the color of your skin. Don't dislike the sound of your voice or the fact that you are tall or short. Learn to love yourself.

6. *Keep on Changing Yourself:* Keep improving yourself. Your complex personality is many-faceted and bound to change. And only you have the freedom to choose how it will change.

7. *Commit Yourself to a Great Cause:* Connect and commit yourself to a cause that, in time, in scope, and in value, transcends your own personal life.

8. *Believe You Can Succeed:* Nothing builds self-esteem faster than success—nothing deflates self-esteem faster than failure.

9. *Dare to Love Yourself:* The truly self-loving person is inwardly secure and so self-assured that he or she is naturally, truly, and sincerely humble. This explains why truly great people are very relaxed and relaxing persons. They put on no airs. They don't need to impress people with their importance. What, after all, is humility? It is not thinking less of oneself; it is thinking more of others.

10. *Constantly Strive to Excel:* Excellence works wonders in strengthening self-esteem. Failure breeds despair.

11. *Help Others Build Self-Esteem:* To achieve a deeper self-esteem yourself, start thinking about people around you who may need to build strong support under their self-esteem.

Having achieved a strong self-esteem, you will find yourself released from an incredible collection of negative tensions. With a stronger and more positive self-esteem, you will be able—better than ever before—to replace inner stress and strain with inner peace, love, power, and creativity.

Building Self-Esteem in Ourselves and Others

There is growing evidence that we are able to love others only when we love ourselves. And in order to improve relationships, one could first develop his or her own self-esteem.

But there is another way to improve relationships and increase self-esteem at the same time, and that is to build self-esteem in ourselves by building the self-esteem in others. Let me illustrate.

Each semester at Brigham Young University I teach a course on preparation for marriage. One of our lessons is on self-esteem. I give the students an assignment called "Building Esteem in Others."[9] I highly recommend this exercise to husbands and wives.

The students choose a friend, a roommate, fiancé, spouse (if they are married), or family member. For seven days they are to practice building the esteem of that person without the person's knowing about it. My students are encouraged to withhold criticism, complaints, interruptions, corrections, or directions for one week. They are to express genuine appreciation often and also touch the person in nondemanding and unobtrusive ways at least once each time they are together. They are also to choose three or four things the person would probably like done during the week and then do them.

At the conclusion of the seven days my students report on their experiences. Invariably, the students report that when they help and assist others, their own self-esteem increases.

What we have learned is the scriptural concept of finding oneself by losing oneself in the service of others. (See Matthew 16:25; Mark 8:35; Luke 9:24.)

LDS Insights on Self-Esteem

It is impressive to me that our Church leaders have been aware of the importance of self-respect and self-esteem for some time. President Harold B. Lee spoke on self-respect in the October 1973 general conference.[10] This address is well worth reading. In the October 1974 general conference, President Ezra Taft Benson gave a talk entitled "Do Not Despair." He noted:

> We live in an age when, as the Lord foretold, men's hearts are failing them, not only physically but in spirit. (See D&C 45:26.) Many are giving up heart for the battle of life. Suicide ranks as a major cause of the deaths to college students. As the showdown between good and evil approaches with its accompanying trials and tribulations, Satan is increasingly striving to overcome the Saints with despair, discouragement, despondency, and depression.
>
> Yet, of all people, we as Latter-day Saints should be the most optimistic and the least pessimistic. . . . To help us from being overcome by the devil's designs of despair, discouragement, depression, and despondency, the Lord has provided at least a dozen ways which, if followed, will lift our spirits and send us on our way rejoicing.

I would recommend that you read his entire address, which was printed in the November 1974 *Ensign* on pages 65-67. But in summary, Elder Benson recommended the following:

1. *Repentance.* Despair, he noted, often comes because of iniquity (see Moroni 10:22), and wickedness does not result in happiness. (Alma 41:10.) Jesus admonished those laden with despair to come unto him, and he would make their burden light. (Matthew 11:28-30.)

2. *Prayer.* Persistent prayer is essential to well-being. "Pray always, that you may come off conqueror." (D&C 10:5.)

3. *Service.* "To lose yourself in righteous service to others," Elder Benson noted, "can lift your sights and get your mind off personal problems, or at least put them in proper focus." (See Mosiah 2:17.)

4. *Work.* Work is a blessing, not our doom. Retirement from work has depressed many a man and hastened his death. We should work at taking care of the spiritual, mental, social, and

physical needs of ourselves and those whom we are charged to help. We should not be idle. (See D&C 88:124.) And work, Elder Benson observed, is not just manual labor but includes missionary endeavors, family genealogy, and temple work, as well as magnifying Church assignments.

5. *Health.* We were given the Word of Wisdom (D&C 89) because the condition of the physical body affects the spirit. We should get adequate rest (D&C 88:124) and not work beyond our capabilities (D&C 10:4; Mosiah 4:27). We should be mindful of the kinds and amounts of foods we eat. (D&C 49:18-19; 59:16-20; 89:5-17.) Elder Benson encouraged us to have frequent physical examinations as a safeguard for good health, and to get adequate exercise. (See D&C 89:20.) Wholesome recreation is also part of our religion. (See D&C 136:28.)

6. *Reading.* Reading, and particularly reading the scriptures and words of living and ancient prophets can edify and uplift us. "Reading," Elder Benson noted, ". . . can give direction and comfort in an hour when one is down."

7. *Blessings.* In many instances it is particularly helpful to seek a blessing under the hands of a priesthood holder. Even the Prophet Joseph Smith once sought and received a blessing of solace from his close friend and counselor, Brigham Young. Fathers should watch for the opportunity to give such blessings to wives and children. In addition, reading one's patriarchal blessing during discouraging times can often provide encouragement and direction.

8. *Fasting.* Periodic fasting can help clear the mind and strengthen both the body and spirit. And to make fasting more fruitful, Elder Benson suggests that it be coupled with prayer, meditation, minimal physical labor, and reading and pondering the scriptures.

9. *Friends.* True friends can be particularly helpful by listening to your concerns, sharing your joys and sorrows, and, when appropriate, giving counsel. Joseph Smith noted, "How sweet the voice of a friend is; one token of friendship from any source what-

ever awakens and calls into action every sympathetic feeling."[11]

10. *Music.* Inspiring music may fill the soul with heavenly thoughts, move one to righteous actions, or speak peace to the soul. Memorizing or singing the hymns of Zion can crowd out debilitation, evil, or depressive thoughts.

11. *Endurance.* Once when George A. Smith was very ill, the Prophet Joseph visited him. Elder Smith later reported, "He told me I should never get discouraged, whatever difficulties might surround me. If I were sunk into the lowest pit of Nova Scotia and all the Rocky Mountains piled on top of me, I ought not to be discouraged, but hang on, exercise faith, and keep up good courage, and I should come out on the top of the heap."[12] The Lord told Joseph Smith, "Thine adversity and thine afflictions shall be but a small moment; and then, if thou endure it well, God shall exalt thee on high." (D&C 121:7-8.)

12. *Goals.* Every accountable child of God needs to set goals, both long and short range, in four main areas: spiritual, mental, physical, and social. Pressing forward toward a desired goal can soon put despondency out of mind. And once a goal is accomplished, other appropriate ones can be set.

In conclusion, Elder Benson noted that there is no problem we confront that cannot be withstood with the aid of the Lord. (See 1 Corinthians 10:13.) We can rise above the enemies of despair, depression, discouragement, and despondency by remembering that God provides righteous alternatives.

Self-Esteem Is Vitally Important

In 1979 I was one of six on a curriculum writing committee for the Church. We were asked to write something to prepare single Latter-day Saints for marriage in the temple. We eventually wrote *Foundations for Temple Marriage,* a Sunday School manual with twelve lessons, which is now in use. The first lesson we wrote was on self-esteem, and we included the following quotation by Elder Hartman Rector, Jr.:

> Self-esteem is vitally important to successful performance. Self-esteem is different than conceit—conceit is the weirdest disease in the world. It makes

everyone sick except the one who has it. It is immensely important that you only feel good about yourself. I am sure that you can only feel good about yourself if you are on the way to reaching your potential. I am positive also that no one can be emotionally or physically healthy unless he is keeping the commandments and rendering unto God the things that are God's. I did not say that this obedience would also make you satisfied with your every performance—I seldom am; I'm sure I can improve my performance in the job. But when I'm on the Lord's side, keeping the basic commandments, I feel good about me, I esteem myself as a worthy child of God, and I find I am very positive.[13]

A Unique Teaching Experience

While writing this book I had an unusual experience with the concept of self-esteem. I had been asked to teach the Gospel Doctrine class in our ward, and the subject matter was from the Old Testament. I hesitated when accepting the assignment because I didn't then know much about the Old Testament. I accepted and struggled each week to teach the concepts and doctrines in a way that gave relevancy to modern living, something I have committed myself to doing in my role as college professor as well as Sunday School teacher.

One particular Sunday the lesson was on Jeremiah, and I thought all during the previous week (as I usually did) about the lesson. Finally, on Sunday morning at 3:00 A.M. I arose and once more read the assigned reading material. I was particularly impressed with Jeremiah's call to be a prophet. He was to do it without the support of a wife and children. In addition, his immediate family turned against him during his prophetic ministry. He was truly alone.

When he was called, he told the Lord of his unworthiness and supposed inability to accept the call. (Jeremiah 1:6-9.) One might say at that point he had low self-esteem.

To counteract Jeremiah's lack of confidence, the Lord told him something rather remarkable. It was, in essence, "Before thou wast born, I knew thee." (See Jeremiah 1:5.) Jeremiah had a premortal identity and association with the Lord. And the Lord was simply reminding Jeremiah of this at the time of his call.

At that early Sunday morning hour, it occurred to me that the Lord knew not only Jeremiah before he was born, but each of us who came to mortality. He knew us personally, as he knew Jeremiah, as his own son or daughter. And I decided that would be my message in Sunday School later that morning.

By my side at that early hour was a book by Truman G. Madsen, *The Highest in Us*. In this book Dr. Madsen relates a fascinating story I later told to my Sunday School class. The story is by James Hilton and was taken from his book *Random Harvest.*

This story is about a wealthy Englishman, Sir Charles Rainier, who goes to war and is shell-shocked in the midst of a battle. His memory is blotted out—he can't even recall his name. He is returned to England and committed to an asylum, where he and others hope he will eventually remember who he is.

One day Sir Charles walks away from the asylum and meets an English girl in a nearby shop. The beautiful young woman, Paula, recognizes him as a man from the asylum who has forgotten his identity. To make a short story even shorter, they become fond of each other and eventually marry.

Sir Charles returns to Liverpool and is struck by a taxi. The memory of his former identity returns, but he loses his memory from the moment of the shell shock. He no longer remembers Paula or any of the subsequent events. He later returns to the home he had before the war, becomes successful in business, and runs for Parliament.

Paula eventually learns of Sir Charles's circumstances and travels to Liverpool. She is hired to be his secretary. He often wonders where he has seen Paula before and later marries her for the second time. Now Sir Charles has two identities while being married to the same woman, but Paula never reveals his second identity.

A few years later, Sir Charles returns to Melbridge, the same community where he spent time in the asylum after the war. Knowing he is going to be there, Paula secretly arranges to arrive in Melbridge at the same time. Sir Charles walks by the asylum, and memories begin to return. He remembers the gates and the little shop where he met Paula. He eventually walks by the cottage where he and Paula used to live. The surroundings are familiar. He opens the door and looks around. It all starts to return.

By this time Paula has come and is standing behind him. She wants to call to him but doesn't know whether to address him as Charles or as Smithy, the name he had when they were first married. He turns around and looks at Paula. She pauses, takes the risk, and says "Smithy!"

For a moment he is confused, but as she breaks into tears his whole past returns. They rush to embrace, and that's the end of the story. It is also the beginning.

Dr. Madsen comments:

> We, too, are wealthy and titled "Englishmen." We once dwelt in the scintillating presence of the Eternal Father. . . . Like Sir Charles Rainier in the story, we were sent into the mortal world clear in the vision of how high were the stakes. There is real evidence that some shrank from that momentous decision. And we, too, have been shell-shocked.
>
> We do not know our own name, rank, and serial number. Even the memory of a perfect language, with its grace and ease and instant communicative power is gone. Here, (mortality) we do indeed stammer and stutter in speech as in conduct, groping our way to self-understanding and feeling at times, even in the midst of helpful people, "strangers and foreigners." We yearn to belong. Only when we are touched by the Spirit do we overcome, for a fleeting time, our memory imprisonment. Then, as Joseph F. Smith puts it, "we are lighted up with the glory of our former home."
>
> My testimony to you is that you have come literally "trailing clouds of glory." No amount of mortal abuse can quench the divine spark. If you only knew who you are and what you did and how you earned the privileges of mortality, and not just mortality but of this time, this place, this dispensation, and the associates that have been meant to cross and intertwine with your lives; if you knew now the vision you had then of what this trial, this probation (what in my bitter moments I call this spook alley) of mortality could produce, would produce; if you knew the latent infinite power that is locked up and hidden for your own good now—if you knew these things you would never again yield to any of the putdowns that are a dime a dozen in our culture today. Everywhere pessimism, everywhere suspicion, everywhere the denial of the worth and dignity of man.[14]

In my class that morning we reviewed Jeremiah 1:5 and discussed how the Lord knew him, and us, before our mortal birth. I related the story of Sir Charles Rainier. We discussed the fourteenth chapter of John which tells of "another comforter" the Holy Ghost, who will "bring all things to [our] remembrance" (John 14:26), including our premortal, spiritual identity.

I then asked Sister Eva Anderson, who has one of the most clear and impressive singing voices I have ever heard, if she would be willing to sing "O My Father." I told the class that they had all heard or sung the hymn numerous times before, but that I wanted them to hear it again after what we had discussed that morning. I wish I could describe the feeling we had as she sang that beautiful hymn that day. And there were few dry eyes, including my own, when she concluded singing.

We then had a closing prayer and dismissed the class. This was, indeed, a unique learning experience, as much for the teacher as for the class members. For just a few minutes we all had a glimpse of our first estate, of that "more exalted sphere" from which we all have wandered. And who could have low self-esteem with such knowledge!

8

HOMEMAKING

Many husbands who responded to my *Deseret News* survey indicated that they expected their wives to be adequate mothers. (See chapter 4.) And they also indicated they wanted their wives to be good homemakers. If a mother neglects her home and children, it subsequently affects her marriage. It appears, therefore, that when a woman marries she has three important roles: wife, mother, and homemaker.

Shock Absorber or Shock Producer?

In his book *Future Shock*, Alvin Toffler comments on the numerous and abrupt changes families may face in the future. In chapter 11, "The Fractured Family," he notes, "The family has been called the 'giant shock absorber' of society—the place to which the bruised and battered individual returns after doing battle with the world, the one stable point in an increasingly flux-filled environment. As the super-industrial revolution unfolds, this 'shock absorber' will come in for some shocks of its own."[1]

Toffler then documents what he believes to be some of the major changes in family life in the future. It may be that the family of the future could become a giant shock producer. That is, rather than *cushion* the harsh reality of life for family members, the family of the future may well *produce* a major portion of their trauma, physical and emotional. Making or keeping the home a refuge from the world, a giant shock absorber, is what homemaking is all about.

Christopher Lasch, professor of history at the University of Rochester, has noted in his recent book *Haven in a Heartless World*, "As business, politics, and diplomacy grow more savage and warlike, men seek a haven in private life, in personal relations, above all in the family—the last refuge of love and decency. Domestic life, however, seems increasingly incapable of providing these comforts. Hence the undercurrent of anxiety that runs through the vast growing body of commentary on the state of the family. Does the family still provide a haven in a heartless world? Or do the very storms out of which the need for such a haven arises threaten to engulf the family as well?"[2]

While both husbands and wives share an equal responsibility in providing this haven for themselves and their children, it seems obvious that the wife and mother has the major responsibility for maintaining stability.

Food Preparation

Perhaps we have not come very far from the days when men hunted and killed the food and women prepared it for consumption. But it is obvious that many women are going to work to help purchase food and other necessities of life. It is also evident that most husbands still expect their wives to prepare and serve the meals. While husbands, on occasion, may warm up some hot dogs or fix a few other simple meals, wives likely will prepare and serve 90 percent of the meals in most homes. And a wife who cannot or will not prepare nutritious meals on a regular basis will harm her family and ultimately her marriage in several ways.

One young man who was about to marry wrote:

Dear Dr. Barlow:

How important is it for a young woman to know how to cook before she gets married? I am engaged and plan to marry in December. Our only major problem is that my fiancée hasn't had much experience cooking but thinks it won't matter. She says we can eat out a lot and buy food that she will just have to warm and serve. Is this realistic for newlyweds?

I responded:

It is important for all married couples to dine out periodically just to be alone and give the wife a rest. And buying precooked foods can be advantageous once in a while. But a steady diet of it can get monotonous. Preprocessed foods also cost much more than food you buy and prepare yourself.

I have always maintained that every couple needs at least three books when they get married: a finance book, a sex book, and a cook book. It seems to me your future bride is desperately in need of the latter.

Married couples must establish many daily routines, including cooking, eating, and cleaning up. Most couples eat over one thousand meals a year together, and I can think of few things that would take the zip out of marriage more than sitting down together to one thousand ill-prepared, unappetizing meals each year.

Sooner or later, I think your wife will have to or want to get involved in food purchasing and preparation. Some would like to ignore the importance of such realities as cooking, but it is impossible to do so.

Home Maintenance

Jerome Chodorov gave this advice to contemporary wives: "I'll tell you the real secret of how to stay married. Keep the cave clean. They [husbands] want the cave clean and spotless. Air-conditioned, if possible. Sharpen his spear, and stick it in his hand when he goes out in the morning to spear the bear. And when the bear chases him, console him when he comes home at night. Tell him what a big brave man he is. And then hide the spear so he doesn't fall over it and stab himself."[3] Such are the secrets of life.

Psychologists are beginning to understand how structure, order, space, color, and texture affect our lives for better or for worse. This is particularly true of our homes. In fact, Winston Churchill once noted, "We shape our buildings and afterward our buildings shape us."

In his article "Housing Affects Family," Dr. Jay Schvaneveldt, Professor of Family and Human Development at Utah State University noted, "The sociological importance and value of the family may be definitely enhanced or injured by the type of dwelling." Dr. Schvaneveldt then noted the extensive research that affirms that the type of house a family lives in greatly influences the general character and attitudes of the inhabitants.

He continued:

> It is well accepted that people design homes to project their feelings and lifestyles, but less common and less understood is that homes design people. Our research shows that if you are really interested in how people live and relate with one another, study them in their homes. It is in the home that people love, fight, and socialize with each other. The home is a sanctuary for reprieve or a prison of hostility. People feel that the real "me" can function in the home. They do not have to be on stage, perform or present a certain self in their home. The house serves as a depository for family themes. History, ritual and the ongoing activity of multiple family members. Hobbies and creations most often occur in the home. Historically, the home also served as a center for the critical life events—birth, illness and death.
>
> Light, space, windows and a home in good repair are significantly related to happiness and good family life. Crowding is related to poor mental health, poor child care, poor physical health and personal stress due to a lack of privacy.[4]

It is always amazing to me what a coat of paint will do not only to a room but to the attitudes of those who live in it. I don't know if it is the smell of fresh paint, the cleanliness of the new walls, or the actual color that gives such good feelings, but a good paint brush and gallon of paint can do a great deal for both rooms and marriages.

Not all wives need to be experts in interior decorating. But perhaps we have not given enough attention to how the physical structure, arrangement of space, lighting, and colors of our homes affect our lives. And perhaps we have not investigated how we could better use these dimensions of our homes to make them more attractive and liveable.

It also became apparent, as I read the many questionnaires that husbands returned to me, that one common expectation was that a wife be able to manage and run an orderly home. This does not necessarily imply that a wife has to do it alone. But the simple truth is that a poorly managed home affects not only husbands, but wives and children as well.

Relief Society president Barbara Smith has noted, "An orderly home is conducive to happiness. But the achievement and maintenance of order, while it is the primary responsibility of the mother, should be the concern of the whole family. And when a mother is required to work outside the home, the cooperation of the family, of the whole household, is often critical."[5]

Whenever I discuss the importance of an orderly home in my marriage seminars, some of the wives become a little defensive. They remind me that *orderly* and *clean* are relative terms and that one could devote his or her entire day to making a house clean and orderly and still not have it acceptable to others. And I know what they mean. Susan works hard at keeping our home orderly, and yet our six children can come home and in minutes make our home look as if it had had little attention. In our home we have learned to distinguish between clutter and dirt. A house can often become cluttered, as anyone with small children knows. But at the same time it can still be clean.

On the other hand, some wives spend too much time on the orderliness of the home and ignore other important needs. One of our friends is very concerned about her kitchen and will not let anyone see any dirty dish on the table or sink. When she has dirtied a dish she cleans it and puts it back on the shelf. (She also will not let anyone see her during the day without her hair immaculately combed.)

On a similar note, one husband conveyed to me his concern about his wife's well-meaning attempts to keep the house orderly and clean. He simply said that having a perfectly clean house did not matter that much to him, and he wished she would spend more time doing things for herself rather than trying to have a spotless home at all times for her family.

When I was attending Florida State University and working on my doctoral degree, I took a course on families in the United States. Each student had to select a particular group or family type and write a research paper on it. I chose the Shakers, a name given to the United Society of Believers in Christ's Second Appearing, also called the Millennial Church. I learned that the Shakers (there are fewer than a dozen members left) are known for many things, one of which is their orderliness. Their motto is, "A place for everything and everything in its place." This motto could well be adopted by Latter-day Saints, and I have been impressed that orderliness and cleanliness are frequently mentioned in Latter-day Saint scripture. In fact, the Book of Mormon notes that a lack of order is one trait of depravity. (Moroni 9:18.) Elsewhere in the Book of Mormon, King Benjamin admonishes, "All things must be done in order." (Mosiah 4:27.) In the Doctrine and Covenants we read, "Organize yourselves; prepare every needful thing; and establish a house, even a house of prayer, a house of fasting, a house of faith, a house of learning, a house of glory, a house of order, a house of God." (D&C 88:119.) The Lord also counseled, "Set in order your houses; keep slothfulness and uncleanness far from you." (D&C 90:18.)

So how do you keep a home in order? Susan has found one book on this topic to be extremely helpful. It is entitled *Confessions of an Organized Housewife.* The author, Deniece Schofield, observes:

> In my role as a homemaker, my main goal is to provide for my family a tidy, comfortable home. I want to make home a place where we all want to be. Confusion and disorder drive people away. Everyone wants to be surrounded by a peaceful atmosphere. . . . Children, as well as adults, feel more secure in a home that is consistent and orderly. They know what to expect and what is expected. How can we teach our children responsibility if we fail to be responsible in our homemaking roles?
>
> The only way to achieve this goal [of peaceful surroundings] is through organization! Yes, there will be times when things are a mess, but when the underlying things are in order, the surface messes are easy to clean up. When everything has a well-defined place, it doesn't take long to put things back where they belong. So, you see, the chaos will never last for long and I can quickly return my family and myself to peaceful surroundings.[6]

It may also be that the degree of spirituality in a home is directly related to the cleanliness of the surroundings. (See chapter 2.) The Lord has admonished us to "cease to be unclean." (D&C 88: 124.) And we are told that the Lord's presence and glory will not come into unclean surroundings. (D&C 94:9; 97:15.) Uncleanliness may include more than sin. It may also have something to do with the surroundings in which we live. This may be one reason our temples are kept so clean, both inside and out, and why those who enter are required to maintain certain dress and grooming standards.

Elder Richard L. Evans has noted:

> There is a word that has within it some wonderful possibilities for personal peace, for safety, for self-respect, and the word is called "clean." Clean hands, clean hearts, clean homes; clean water, clean air, clean clothes—clean minds, clean morals—what a wonderful word! *The mind so often follows environment—and the cycle reverses itself, as the environment follows the mind.* We can have a hopeful outlook in almost anything, if we commit ourselves to cleanliness. . . . That "cleanliness is next to godliness" is not just an old adage but a real fact to face: cleanliness of thought, of person, of dress, of speech. There is not only "the strength of being clean," but peace and safety and self-respect. . . . God help us to commit ourselves to cleanliness.[7] (Italics added.)

When Mothers Work Too Much

It is my firm contention that the vast majority of Latter-day Saint women are very conscientious about their responsibilities as homemakers and mothers. In many cases they may be too conscientious. In fact, this may be why some women become discouraged and experience what has recently been identified as "homemaker burnout."

There has been much talk recently about burnout in many professions. This phenomenon has been described as a debilitating psychological condition affecting individuals who work in high stress situations for prolonged periods of time. It has only been during the past year or so that we have begun to give much attention to burnout in the home.

David Willis and Harold Fondren, both counselors in the LDS Social Services, have written an article entitled "Burnout in the Home,"[8] in which they note that burnout can often be misdiagnosed as depression and suggest that symptoms of homemaker burnout include irritability, exhaustion, desperate measures to deal with routine problems, impatience, distrust, resignation, withdrawal, apathy, negativism, lack of attentiveness, cynicism, decreased energy and motivation, and an increased emotional distance from husband and children.

According to Willis and Fondren, homemaker burnout has been found to be particularly high in the following kinds of homes:

1. Homes with young, inexperienced homemakers who consistently compare themselves with older and seemingly better women and mothers. Some young mothers try to live up to the myth of the "perfect mother in Zion," which is how they perceive some other LDS women.

2. Homes with many children and inflexible, autocratic fathers.

3. Homes where husbands always find time for "important" Church meetings but rarely have time to be with their children and wives consistently.

4. Homes where the homemaker does not know exactly what is expected of her and where communication of family rules is unclear.

5. Homes where there is little autonomy for the homemaker and few opportunities for individuality or innovation.

6. Homes where the homemaker is overly conscientious and has too high an expectation of herself.

7. Homes where the homemaker has not learned to set priorities, let some things go temporarily, or feels guilty when she does set priorities but is unable to attend to all of them equally.

David Willis and Harold Fondren note:

> It is our feeling that examples of low resource allocation for support of the homemaker are found in most homes where burnout has occurred. This may be

evidenced by the husband coming home from work, and rather than relieving his wife, saying he needs to rest. So he reads the paper, eats dinner, has a five-minute interview with the kids, goes to his ward basketball game, then attends his leadership meeting. He returns home refreshed and invigorated but returns home to and is confused by an angry wife—a wife who has probably been taught to sublimate her needs to that of her husband and children, and is angry because of these feelings of anger directed towards her husband, especially since he is a "nice" man and faithful in the Church.[9]

The authors suggest that Latter-day Saints could do more to support homemakers in addition to the traditional flower on Mother's Day. Each stake might do more to encourage women's sports by providing the facilities and also the encouragement to participate. Latter-day Saints might sponsor mother-daughter outings, mother overnight campouts, and women's conferences. We do these things for husbands and fathers, so why not for wives and mothers? More might also be done to help husbands realize that parenthood for Latter-day Saints is a responsibility that should be equally shared rather than implying that mothers have the total or near-total responsibility for rearing the children.

Willis and Fondren state in conclusion:

> Our recommendations are based upon this supposition: To meet the needs of her children, a mother's needs must be met, and therefore the mother's needs must be met basically by the husband.
>
> It is our contention that while some women may exhibit characteristics of rebellion or lack of respect to their husband or priesthood leader, most of these are probably reactions to a lack of being listened to, understood, and/or appreciated by the husband or priesthood leader. Most women would follow a husband or priesthood leader who (1) understood and listened to her, (2) understood her needs, (3) showed and expressed consistent appreciation, and (4) allocated more resources to support her in her role as a homemaker.[10]

Working outside the Home

If a Latter-day Saint homemaker decides to seek outside employment, there are several things she should consider.

In our Church, much, if not all of the deliberations about working mothers has focused on the impact it may have on the children. And this is a crucial concern. In her book *The Two-*

Paycheck Marriage, Caroline Bird has written an in-depth report of how women at work are changing life in America.

She documents in her first chapter, "The Exodus to Work," that about 60 percent of married women now are employed outside the home, either part or full time, and appear to want to stay in the labor force. It is not just a temporary trend. In addition, it is projected that by the year 1990 at least 70 percent of married women will be employed. As was found in the General Mills Study of 1981, most wives go to work for economic reasons, but once there, they stay not only for economic reasons but because of the satisfaction often derived from rewarding labor. Latter-day Saints cannot ignore these trends.

But neither can Latter-day Saints ignore findings of Caroline Bird and others about the adjustments required in a marriage and family for a wife to work outside the home. She documents from her research that work does, in fact, affect wives in several areas that should be considered by LDS couples. Bird notes that working wives usually have (1) greater fatigue, (2) less leisure time, (3) power struggles in decision-making, (4) lower standards of household care and maintenance, (5) sexual adjustments in marriage (which incidentally were noted to improve for wives but become worse for husbands), and (6) an effect on children.

On this latter matter, Bird suggests that one might pick his bias and then quote the appropriate research to support that bias. The facts appear to be that (1) some children are definitely harmed by inattentiveness of absent mothers, particularly those who are employed outside the home; (2) some children are affected little, either negatively or positively, by a mother's work outside the home, and (3) some children are positively affected by mothers who work outside the home. Most research falls somewhere in these three categories with much depending on the age of the child, the presence of the father in the absence of the mother, the quality of supervision provided in the mother's absence, the woman's own skills at being a mother (children with inept mothers are often greatly aided by having interaction with more skilled adults), the degree of satisfaction the wife receives from her work, and the feeling the mother has toward herself, her work, her children, and her husband. What effect working has on specific LDS marriages and families depends on these and several other variables.

One of the most relevant findings of Caroline Bird is the enormous amount of time it takes a wife and mother just to operate and maintain a home. She notes:

> It takes a woman more hours a week to run the home than her husband puts in on the average job. This is not an empty boast. Syracuse housewives were averaging 57 hours a week on "purposeful activity performed for providing the goods and services used by the family." The average was 55 hours for a national sample of full-time homemakers who kept time diaries of what they did every 15 minutes in 1966 for the Survey Research Center of the University of Michigan. Updates on these basic studies don't change the surprising conclusion that *full-time homemakers spend just as many hours on their homes and families as they did in the 1920's.*[11] (Italics added.)

So, when a wife and mother goes to work full time, she adds a forty-hour work week (minimum) to the fifty-five to fifty-seven-hour one she already has at home. Even by working half time, she works a minimum of seventy-five hours a week rather than the typical fifty-five to fifty-seven hours.

But, one assumes, when wives go to work, husbands jump right in, come to their rescue, and do much if not most of the housework in her absence. Not so, according to research! In my book *What Wives Expect of Husbands,* I noted that many wives want *help.* And perhaps this is because so many wives are employed outside the home. But husbands do little to help wives in the home whether wives are employed or not. That is the bad news. The good news, however, is that a quiet social revolution is occurring in the United States. Husbands, particularly young ones, are starting to help more around the home.

When a woman adds twenty to forty hours of work outside the home to the fifty-five to fifty-seven she spends maintaining the home, it is little wonder, as Caroline Bird notes in *The Two-*

Paycheck Marriage, that working women experience a significant increase in fatigue, a significant decrease in her own leisure time, and a lower standard of household care and maintenance. She simply has neither the time nor the energy to keep things as they were. These are all important factors to consider.

Dr. Jerry Mason, family finance expert and member of the Family Sciences Department at Brigham Young University (and my next-door office neighbor) raises another matter for Latter-day Saint wives and mothers to consider before they seek and accept employment outside the home. He notes:

> Research indicates that married women seek paid employment outside the home largely because of financial reasons to help support their families. Many families, however, fail to calculate the actual number of net dollars she contributes to the family after subtracting fixed and variable expenses from her salary.
>
> The hypothetical case of an LDS couple listed below illustrates the expenditures a second member of the family could reasonably expect to incur at the present time (1982) if the husband or primary breadwinner is already employed.

Case Study

Suppose an LDS husband earns $20,000 annually and his wife has recently been offered a job for a full-time position that pays $10,000 a year. Two of their three children attend elementary school and the third one would require full-time child care in order for the mother to work. Consider the following:

Salary Offer:		$10,000
Expenditures:		
Federal Income Taxes[12]	$1,400	
State Income Taxes	360	
Social Security Taxes	670	
Tithing	1,000	
Child Care (net of tax credit)	2,800	
Clothing[13]	600	
Personal Care[14]	450	
Food[15]	600	

Transportation[16]	500	
Total Expenditures:		8,380
Discretionary Income:		$1,620

According to Dr. Mason, data for a "typical" family does not perfectly fit most families.[17] If the husband's salary is significantly above $20,000, the wife's financial contribution will probably be minimal. However, if the husband's salary is smaller than $20,000, the wife's contribution may be larger. The progressive structure of the federal and state income tax rate schedules explains such differences. When a wife earns less than $10,000, the family will receive little financial support from her unless the husband's salary is low.

The largest expense usually incurred is child care. Wives who must pay for child care for more than one child if they return to paid employment may find that the family is financially worse off than if she had stayed home. In fact, this is the situation for many families even when not paying child care because the family believes that it is financially better off now that the wife is earning a paycheck. Dr. Mason notes that such families often get into financial trouble using credit to buy items on time that they could not previously afford because they actually have erroneously assumed that they have $10,000 to spend when they have less than $2,000.[18] Since, in many cases, the wife's actual contribution to the family income is insignificant, the budget becomes even less flexible as it stretches to cover these additional installment payments.

Every family is unique. Each one needs to examine the financial impact of a change in the employment role responsibilities of any family member. As the above case study indicates, when an LDS mother has to pay for preschool child care and returns to work, she is not likely to make a significant financial contribution to the family unless her income exceeds $10,000 or her husband's income is considerably below $20,000.

Dr. Mason's observations are noteworthy. He also indicates

that the same expenditures and "costs" must also be applied to a man's salary in determining the actual number of net dollars he contributes to the family's financial support. He, too, pays taxes, tithing, and spends money on clothing, personal care, food, and transportation for him to do what he does to be employed. And for women, it is difficult to place a dollar value on satisfaction derived from worthwhile work both in and outside the home.

But the point is well-taken. Before an LDS couple decides it would be financially profitable for a wife to be employed outside the home for economic reasons, they should carefully examine Dr. Mason's insights.

9

ATTRACTIVENESS

From my *Deseret News* survey, I found that husbands evidently want an attractive wife, as indicated in the Profile of a Loving Wife (appendix B). However, I also found that most wives were attractive to their husbands. Numerous husbands ranked high the item "She is aware that her appearance and physical fitness affect how I feel about her." And notice that the word "affect" is used rather than "cause." But research and opinion aside, simply ask your husband if your appearance and physical fitness are important. His opinion is the only man's that really matters.

A woman from Salt Lake City wrote not long ago and took me to task for saying in my newspaper column that husbands want or appreciate attractiveness in a wife. For my observation, she called me a male chauvinist you-know-what-oinks. The accusation caused me some thought. Was I really the personification of male chauvinism or did I merely comment on a sensitive area in marriage? Is it solely my biased observation or is it a common expectation of many husbands? After more thought, I still believe that attractiveness is important, in fact, very important, to men in marriage. And apparently so do others.

Noted psychologist Dr. Joyce Brothers, in her book *What Every Woman Should Know about Men,* notes, "A poll of more than a thousand young men revealed that personality was more important to them than beauty. Another group of men reported that the most appealing quality in a woman is her ability to show affection. A survey conducted by an advertising agency found that one out of ten men want a woman who first of all will be a good mother. Seven out of ten said that the ideal woman is intelligent, family-oriented, and self-confident. Beauty was way down on their list of desirable qualities."[1]

But then Dr. Brothers observes, "No matter what men say for the record, good looks are what they want most in a woman. You have to remember that there is quite often a difference between what people say and what they really think. Men may not think it sounds correct or intelligent or sophisticated to say that beauty is what appeals to them most, so they tell the interviewer that affection or a good personality or an independent spirit is what they are seeking."[2]

On a similar note, Elaine and G. William Walster observe in their book *A New Look at Love,* "We've all been told countless times from adolescence onward that looks don't count—it's what's inside that matters. But few of us ever bought that idea completely. Looks *shouldn't* count, of course, but we all know that they usually do. Social psychologists have accumulated file-drawers full of evidence that good-looking men and women have a big advantage in the marriage market. Beauty does count."[3]

One study indicated that looks are rated very high by some men. At the College of San Mateo in California, 350 randomly selected men and 350 randomly selected women were asked to write down three qualities they valued most in a date and three qualities they valued most in a marriage partner.

The qualities listed by men as the most valuable in a date were, in rank order: (1) looks, (2) personality, (3) sex appeal, (4) intelligence, and (5) fun, good companionship. The qualities listed by women as the most valued in a man for a date were, in rank order: (1) looks, (2) personality, (3) thoughtfulness, consideration, (4) sense of humor, and (5) honesty.

And what qualities did they desire in a marriage partner?

Men wanted (again in rank order): (1) looks, (2) love, (3) compatibility, (4) sex appeal, (5) and personality. Qualities a woman wanted in a husband were (1) love, (2) honesty, (3) compatibility, (4) understanding, and (5) loyalty, faithfulness.[4]

As you will note, looks or attractiveness was the number one quality a man was seeking in both a date and a wife in this particular study. Was this a biased sample, or were the respondents just a little more honest?

The husbands in my survey indicated that attractiveness is desirable in a marriage partner. So perhaps good looks rank somewhere between "highly important" and "somewhat important" to men.

A Second Opinion

Before you come to the conclusion that I, as a man, am giving too much attention to attractiveness in marriage, you might like a second opinion, this time from a woman. Judith Rasband is a colleague at Brigham Young University who also writes a newspaper column. Recently she wrote the following, which I find intriguing:

> Ann Landers isn't the only one who receives letters from disillusioned spouses. In a letter signed "Can't bear to look any longer," a disheartened husband complained to me about the appearance of his wife of eleven years.
>
> He wrote that she wore the same wrinkled, ragged dresses and "grungy" slacks day after day. Her clothes were all several sizes too small due to her nonstop weight gain (which he remembers began the moment they walked away from the altar).
>
> He said he was tired of telling her to "tuck in the tag end of her straps," which periodically protruded from her neckline. "She used to shave her legs," he lamented, "but no more, and now they look so ugly under her nylons that she will only wear pants or long dresses when we are out in public."
>
> His complaints certainly seem to have some merit, and his wife needs to be completely "recycled," as one of my students puts it. Somewhere between the altar and the diaper pail this weary wife has lost sight of the attractive woman she used to be, as well as the sparkle in her eye and her looks.
>
> Perhaps the demands on her time, energy, and money have caused her to give in to a sloppy appearance. And maybe the pressure of her house and chil-

dren, PTA, church, and the March of Dimes have gotten to be so much that she has just given up. Let's face it, the let-down in personal appearance often starts soon after the ceremony. One young man knew the honeymoon was over when his wife of one week quit curling her hair and wearing her usual makeup along with the perfume he had so often appreciated. She figured she'd won her man, so why bother now?

If you're married you "won" your spouse, in part, because of your appearance and what it said about your personality, your values, hopes and dreams. Dress to win even in your home! Don't continually neglect your appearance or the care you give yourself once the ring is on your finger.

If you don't keep up those important appearances, you take the chance that your partner may become disenchanted, and may even look around for more attractive scenery, making him—or her—a prime target for Cupid's misguided arrows.

Even marriages made in heaven have been known to go sour when one or the other partner lets down on his or her appearance.

If any of this sounds remotely close to home, surprise your special someone with some extra attention to your dress and grooming. Then be sure you follow through long after that. I can almost guarantee the lift it will give you and the heartfelt appreciation and respect that your sweetheart will feel as a result. The compliments will come, and you will know that someone cares.[5]

The importance of trying to look one's best and to be as attractive as possible was also indicated in a letter I received from a wife. She wrote:

> The thing that has kept our marriage vital, better than anything else, happened completely unplanned. I have not always been as careful about my appearance as I should have been. But a few years ago, I decided I would start going to the hair dresser once each week to get my hair done. I did this, and since my hair was now looking so nice, I started putting a little makeup on each morning. It wasn't too long after I started doing this that I noticed my husband, too, was taking more pride in his own appearance—a shower each day and many other things. Our sex life improved, and he expressed his love for me much more often. Our whole marriage just became much more meaningful to both of us.

Some Thoughts on Beauty

Almost everyone today seems to be discontent with some aspect of his or her body. We are either too short or too tall, too thin or too fat. We have too much or too little hair that is too straight, too curly, or too gray. Our eyes are either the wrong color or not in the right position. And our nose is somehow out of proportion. In essence, we do not feel we are among the beautiful people of our country.

But we may also have purchased a bill of goods we neither want or need. Exactly who are the beautiful people, anyway? What are we trying to become?

Usually the supposedly beautiful people portrayed on television, in the movies, or on the covers of magazines are young, extremely beautiful, and very slim. Television advertisements for diet drinks are notorious for depicting such people. Problems frequently arise when we try to be like these beautiful people or want our spouses to be exactly like the ones constantly "packaged" by the mass media.

The reality is that less than 10 percent of the population is actually beautiful by Madison Avenue standards or the standards of television advertisers and fashion magazines. And yet the other 90 percent of us are spending great effort and millions, perhaps billions, of dollars each year to try to be beautiful by these standards.

And the price for many who want such beauty is often extremely high. Many try to be young, beautiful, and slim, but in the process end up being preoccupied, miserable, and usually unbearable to live with. If we do equate beauty with youth, as many do, we fight a losing battle, advertising to the contrary. The reality is that *everyone* ages.

Throughout history, people have had different opinions about beauty and what it is. Socrates called beauty a short-lived tyranny; Plato, a privilege of nature; Theophrastus, a silent cheat; Theocritus, a delightful prejudice; Aristotle, a better recommendation than all the letters in the world; Homer, a glorious gift of nature; and Ovid, a favor bestowed by the gods.

Ninon de Lenclos noted, "That which is striking and beautiful is not always good; but that which is good is always beautiful." And Cervantes warned, "Beauty in a modest woman is like fire at a distance, or a sharp sword beyond reach. The one does not burn, or the other wound those that come not too near them." Similarly, Zimmerman wrote, "Beauty is often worse than wine, intoxicating both the holder and the beholder."

Many have noted that youthful beauty does not last. Shakespeare wrote, "Beauty is but a vain and doubtful good; a shining glass that fadeth suddenly; a flower that dies when it begins to bud, a doubtful good, a gloss, a glass, a flower, lost, faded, broken, dead within an hour."

"Beauty," said T. Adams, "is like an almanac: if it lasts a year, it is well." And Pope mused, "There should be as little merit in loving a woman for her beauty, as a man for his prosperity, both being equally subject to change."

Becoming Attractive

Relatively few people possess the beauty of a Greek god or goddess. And, as noted, not many of us are beautiful by the standards of Madison Avenue. But everyone is or can be attractive in several ways.

One widely read authority on male-female relationships, Alexandra Penney, has commented:

> Very, very, very few people have super bodies and/or flawless faces, and it is important to keep this thought in mind. If you do not, you are likely to fall into some very common traps that you can set for yourself about how you look: the "either I look terrific or I look terrible" trap, the "he's going to notice my blemishes" trap, and the "constant comparison" trap. There will always be a body or a face better than yours, so if you see yourself in these negative terms, you're inevitably going to assume that there is something not right about you, and you'll constantly feel inadequate and unattractive.[6]

If a wife does feel unattractive and uncomfortable about her body, it can affect not only her self-esteem, but also her sexual relationship with her husband. Alexandra Penney notes:

> It is amazing how many of us don't feel attractive or desirable or comfortable with our bodies. . . . Contrary to what the media says, you do not have to be beautiful or to have a perfect body to be truly sexy. Many of our insecurities

and our fears are amplified when we watch TV or go to the movies, or leaf through glossy fashion magazines telling us that people with beautiful faces and beautiful bodies are the ones who are sexy. If you feel that you are sexy, men will feel that you are too. And what does it take to feel sexy? Simply this: the more you are comfortable and at ease with yourself and your body, the more sexy and attractive you will feel. You must feel sexy in order to be sexy.[7]

For a woman to be attractive to her husband, therefore, may mean that she gives as much attention to her attitudes and feelings as she does to her looks. What most husbands want in a wife, apparently, is someone who has confidence in both him and herself.

I was recently interested in some comments by well-known model Cheryl Tiegs. She confided that there were some things about her looks that she really did not like. But she was aware that her eyes were one of her most attractive features. So she had learned how to enhance her eyes with makeup and somewhat played down the other characteristics she deemed less attractive. Cheryl also stated that every woman has some facial qualities that are particularly appealing, and that each woman should learn to enhance those qualities rather than constantly trying to cosmetically hide her other believed flaws.

While I am not the world's greatest authority on what makes people attractive, I have had considerable experience during the past few years with young men and women on several college campuses who want to be attractive to the opposite sex. It has become evident that many who are actually beautiful by today's standards do not date or are not capable of maintaining a sustained relationship. Looks alone won't do it. On the other hand, many young men and women who are average in looks become extremely attractive in one way or another. One of these ways includes learning to smile. A smile is one of the most appealing attributes a person can have. In addition, they learn to make themselves more attractive by the appropriate use of conversation, listening, touch, makeup, and hair and clothing fashion. One of the most effective things a woman can do to become more attractive is simply to update or change her hairstyle and, to some degree, her wardrobe. Both are good investments. Good personal hygiene and the appropriate use of perfumes and lotions have also proven effective.

At least two Church presidents have commented on the importance of beauty and attractiveness in women. As early as 1953 President David O. McKay noted that beauty comes to women from virtuous living. He then stated, "It is not my purpose to discourage efforts to enhance physical beauty. When given by birth, it should be nurtured in childhood, cherished in girlhood, and protected in womanhood. When not inherited, it should be developed and sought after in every legitimate and healthful manner."[8]

A few years ago, President Kimball spoke at Brigham Young University and advised young coeds to "do all in their power to make themselves physically attractive in dress and grooming, mentally in being knowledgeable on many subjects, spiritually in being responsive, emotionally in being genuine and worthy."[9]

President Kimball encouraged young women to make themselves attractive in a variety of ways, one of which was becoming spiritual. Many coeds are still confused by the "sweet spirit" versus the "beautiful tabernacle" controversy at BYU. But many men and women may not realize that spirituality has with it a degree of beauty.

Elder Sterling W. Sill has noted:

> We all know the things that we do to make this body a pleasant habitation. We bathe it and keep it clean; we dress it in the most appropriate clothing. Sometimes we ornament it with jewelry. If we're very wealthy we buy necklaces and bracelets and diamond rings and other things to make this body sparkle and shine and make it a pleasant place. Sometimes we work on it a little bit with cosmetics and eyebrow tweezers. Sometimes we don't help it very much, but we keep working at it all the time.
>
> Now if you think it would be pleasant to be dressed in expensive clothing, what do you think it would be like sometime to be dressed in an expensive body—one that shines like the sun, one that is beautiful beyond all comprehension, with quickened senses, amplified powers of perception, and vastly

increased capacity for love, understanding, and happiness. And we might just keep in mind that God runs the most effective beauty parlor ever known in the world.

Socrates was a very homely man, and he prayed to the Lord and said, "Make me beautiful within." We have all seen plain people who have been made beautiful by the working of a radiant spirituality. A godly spirit will make the plainest body beautiful. Great mental and spiritual qualities transform our bodies into their likeness.[10]

Perhaps this is what Jane Porter had in mind when she wrote, "Beauty of form affects the mind, but then it must not be the mere shell we admire, but the thought that this shell is only the beautiful case adjusted to the shape and value of still a more beautiful pearl within. The perfection of outward loveliness is the soul shining through the crystalline covering."[11]

Weight and Attractiveness

Since deciding to write this book I have debated for some time whether or not to include this section on weight control. So much is said today about weight and diets that seems confusing, contradictory, and sometimes intimidating. Nonetheless, many husbands have indicated that their wives' physical fitness, which includes weight control, did influence how they felt toward them. My challenge, therefore, is how to say that weight really should not and does not matter to many husbands and yet to some it does.

On one occasion, I was just preparing to leave my office when a woman knocked on my door. She told me that her husband had recently told her to lose ten pounds or get out of the house. She had been jogging around the track every day but then stopped one evening and asked herself why. Was she trying to lose weight because her husband demanded it, or was it in her own best interests?

Recently I was talking to a husband and our conversation got around to health and physical fitness. "You know," he said, "I've told my wife if she ever gains too much weight, I will leave her. At that point she can start losing or start looking." He laughed. While my friend may have been a little cavalier in his attitude, I am absolutely convinced that he was, right or wrong, representing the attitude of some husbands.

Another insight on this subject came to me in one of my marriage classes. In a questionnaire I asked, "Does your spouse weigh more now than you would like him or her to weigh?" About 70 percent of my students said no and 30 percent said yes. But the interesting fact was that the wives responded in the same percentage as the husbands.

Most of the couples in these seminars are young, in their middle or late twenties, so we discussed the gradual weight gain that comes to most adults. After graduating from high school, many people gain on an average of one to two pounds a year for the next twenty years. So by the time they are forty years old they are twenty to forty pounds heavier than they were in their early twenties. After some calculating, most of the couples found they were right on schedule for weight gain! We also discussed the fact that after age forty, 30 percent of men and 40 percent of women in the United States are actually obese (20 percent over their ideal weight).[12]

While weight gain does not appear to be a major problem during the early years of marriage, it can and often does become one later. And the habits of good health and physical fitness, or lack of them, developed during the early years of marriage are contributing factors to weight gain later on.

The simple truth is, when a wife or husband is excessively overweight, it can make a difference in marriage. But I do not believe that it is ever grounds for divorce. I am aware, however, o instances where it has been a major contributing cause. Anything that disrupts a marriage is a concern to marriage counselors and educators. And being overweight can adversely affect many dimensions of a marriage, including the sexual relationship.

Weight and Sexual Interaction in Marriage

In their book *The Act of Marriage, a Christian Guide to Sexual Love,* Tim and Beverly LaHaye note:

An attractive but grossly overweight president of a Christian women's club engaged me [Tim] in conversation at a luncheon where I was to speak on "How to Get Your Husband to Treat You Like a Queen." After ten years of marriage she still found sex to be repulsive.

Upon further questioning I discovered that she had not always been overweight, but had gained seventy pounds during her last pregnancy and was unable to lose them. Not surprisingly, she had lost interest in sex and found orgasm impossible for the first time in her married life. With the increase in weight she experienced a decreased self-image. For the first time she was embarrassed to undress in front of her husband.

When I convinced her that her love life would improve and her orgasmic capability would return with the loss of weight (not to mention greater energy, health and self-acceptance), she decided to follow my advice and make an appointment with a weight specialist. Within nine months I received a letter telling me that she had seen improvement in four months and that her love life now was back to normal. She had lost sixty pounds of those demotivating pounds.[13]

I have also had many married couples tell me that their sexual lives improved when either or both lost unnecessary and unwanted weight. And other dimensions of the relationship can also improve. I read not long ago about a study done on weight gain and loss at Utah State University. John E. Gibson indicated that with increasing weight, both men and women reported decreasing self-acceptance, lack of confidence, and loss of self-esteem. He also reported that these people were high in emotionality, more easily upset, and more subject to feelings of depression.[14]

The Cholesterol Kingdom

Being overweight can also seriously affect physical health. And if being overweight is detrimental to health, what implications does this have for Latter-day Saints? Since the early days of our Church, we have become known for the Word of Wisdom which, in general, encourages good health. We meticulously avoid alcohol, tobacco, tea, and coffee for health reasons. But what about being overweight?

Not long ago, my eleven-year-old son, Brian, came home and asked, "Dad, do you know where overweight Mormons go when they die?" I took the bait and said no. He grinned and said, "The cholesterol kingdom!"

What he said in jest does give cause for thought. Should Latter-day Saints have greater concern about physical fitness and weight control? I was interested not long ago in a statement by Dr. Jean Meyer, one of the noted nutrition experts in the world. He observed that being fifty to one hundred pounds overweight could have the equivalent impact on the body of smoking one pack of cigarettes a day.[15] While no upstanding Latter-day Saint would ever think of smoking cigarettes, he or she might ignore other health hazards such as excessive weight gain.

Do we have more than our fair share of weight problems in the Church? Some think so. A few months ago I attended a seminar at the Hotel Utah in Salt Lake City on family life, and a noted authority on weight control, who was not LDS, spoke on this very topic. He gave three reasons why he believed many Latter-day Saints are overweight: (1) The thin Mormon pioneers died during the past century trying to get to Utah, creating a hereditary predisposition to weight problems. (He didn't smile as he said this, but I had a chuckle or two.) (2) Mormons are physically less active than others because of the many Church meetings they sit in. He estimated that active Mormons are 11 percent more sedentary because of this. (3) Mormons do not smoke cigarettes, which has been known to keep weight down but is also detrimental to health. I could have added: (4) Mormons have an apparent preoccupation with calorie-laden foods at many of our Church activities.

All of these are food for thought (no pun intended), but I recently heard something else that concerned me even more. On KSL Radio in Salt Lake City is a call-in program called Public Pulse. On July 29, 1982, Dr. James Mason, a public health official in Utah, was the guest. A caller asked him if there is more obesity in Utah than elsewhere. Dr. Mason commented that as far as he can determine, it is not statistically significant. But he added that it is approaching significance! Put another way, we do not at the present time seem to have more of a weight problem in our state than in others, but we are heading in that direction.

The Word of Wisdom Reexamined

If being overweight is a major health concern, why hasn't the Lord revealed something about it? The fact is, he has. In the eighty-ninth section of the Doctrine and Covenants, the Word of Wisdom, he revealed that certain foods were to be used in their season, "all these to be used with prudence." (Verse 11.) He also indicated that meat was to be used "sparingly." (Verse 12.) In August 1831, the Lord revealed to the Prophet Joseph Smith that He had given a variety of foods to mankind to use for a variety of purposes. All dieters ought to read section 59, which says that food was given "to please the eye and to gladden the heart; . . . for taste and for smell, to strengthen the body and to enliven the soul." (Verses 18-19.) Nowhere do I read that the Lord intended us to exist only on lettuce and cottage cheese.

But the Lord did indicate we should not eat too much. He stated that food was given to be used "with judgment, not to excess, neither by extortion." (D&C 59:20.) Extortion, in this sense, means not to abuse or misuse the body with food. In essence, we are encouraged not to overeat.

Not all excess weight is gained from overeating. (See "Running Away from It All" by S. Scott Zimmerman, *Ensign*, February 1981, pages 28-33.) But the truth is that many of us do overeat. On this theme, President Brigham Young said in 1868, "The Americans, as a nation are killing themselves with vices and high living. As much as a man ought to eat in half an hour they swallow in three minutes, gulping down their food like the canine quadruped under the table, which, when a chunk of meat is thrown down to it, swallows it before you can say 'twice.' If you want a reform, carry out the advice I have just given you. Dispense with your multitudinous dishes, and, depend upon it, you will do much towards preserving your families from sickness, disease and death."[16]

Elsewhere he noted, "Suppose I happen to say 'Come, wife, let us have a good dinner today;' what does she get? Pork and beef boiled, stewed, roasted, and fried, potatoes, onions, cabbage, and turnips, custard, eggs, pies of all kinds, cheese, and sweet-meats. Now grant that I and my wife sit down and overload our stomachs, until we feel the deleterious effects of it from the crowns of our heads to the soles of our feet, the whole system [body] is disturbed in its operations, and is ready to receive and impart disease."[17]

Some LDS Insights on the Human Body

While Latter-day Saints should strive to have healthy bodies as encouraged by the Word of Wisdom, we should not get caught up in the contemporary clamor that our individual worth is determined by a certain physique or body size. *All* individuals have worth regardless of body type! (See D&C 18:10.) *All* physical bodies, regardless of size, shape, appearance, condition, or color, are valued. And gaining one is an essential purpose of coming to mortality. Paul noted that the human body is a temple of God (1 Corinthians 3:16-17), and temples throughout the world are found in assorted sizes and shapes. Yet, all are temples.

Perhaps we have become so preoccupied with dieting, exercising, and losing weight that we sometimes forget the inherent worth of a person regardless of how much he or she weighs or how far he or she can jog. We begin to judge ourselves by our second estate rather than our first estate identity. In many ways, we have accepted the world's standard of who or what is attractive, desirable, or acceptable.

In their excellent book *Getting to Know the Real You*, Sterling G. and Richard G. Ellsworth discuss the physical versus the spiritual identity of men and women. I highly recommend their book to Latter-day Saints who would like a gospel perspective on self-esteem and the physical body. In their book they note three distinct trends:

1. We can do the wrong thing for the wrong reason.
2. We can do the right thing for the wrong reason.
3. We can do the right thing for the right reason.[18]

With these three ideas in mind, we can make some interesting observations about weight control, exercise, dieting, and attitudes toward the body.

A person might abuse or desecrate his or her body in an extreme way to lose weight, appear thin, or gain respect and attention from others. Such a person might abuse the body by excessive fasting, bulimia (splurge and purge), or extremely stressful or strenous exercise. He or she might eat inadequately or seldom and then only eat certain "diet foods" that may be lacking in essential nutrients. This is a good example of doing the wrong thing for the wrong reason.

Another person, however, may exercise moderately, cut down on the amount of food eaten, refrain from non-nutritive eating, and, in general, strive to keep the body healthy. But the motive in this case is also for peer acceptance and approval. Such a person may do so to retain youthfulness, believing that a youthful body is of more worth than one that is not. That person may want to be part of the diet-drink generation or to show others sheer will power and self-control. He or she may dress in extreme fashion, often at high cost, and ornament the body so as to be accepted. This is an example of doing the right thing (maintaining a healthy body) for the wrong reason (social and peer approval, which supposedly determines self-worth).

What would be, then, an example of doing the right thing for the right reason? According to Ellsworth and Ellsworth, it would be to maintain a healthy body so the body can serve the needs of the spirit where, according to LDS theology, the real identity is found. One of the authors notes:

> I know a young girl who tried to kill herself because she wasn't accepted into a certain sorority. . . . She didn't have the right shape, or the right size, or the right face to suit that society. She was terribly hurt because her healthy clean young body didn't satisfy some others' designs. . . .
>
> How worthless she felt she was! And how confused she *really* was, and hopeless! She had come to think that her body was her self. If her body was acceptable, then she was acceptable; if it failed, she had failed. But how absolutely wrong she was. Her body was really external to her real [spiritual] self. It

> was like a car, a house, or a suit of clothing. A body exists to serve the spirit that dwells in it. It is external and of the world; it is a servant to the internal reality of the soul. . . . How vital it is then to have a correct self-concept! How important it is to our mental health to know our real selves, to recognize the proper purposes and places of internal and external values![19]

For health reasons, Latter-day Saint husbands and wives should maintain a proper weight and be physically fit. This is consistent with our philosophy of good health contained in the Word of Wisdom. But *never* should we allow our worth and identity to be determined only by the appearance of the physical body. Among the teachings we have to offer is the inherent worth of each individual. Truly, the worth of each soul is great! (D&C 18:10.)

FINAL COMMENTS

As we conclude this book, allow me to make a few observations on one or two matters.

Highs and Lows in Marriage

If asked to do so, almost every married couple could recall some difficult moments they have had during their years of marriage. And perhaps we do think about these times often. But the difficult times do not necessarily mean we loved each other less. It may simply mean that such times were not as good as others before or since.

One of the interesting dynamics of couples contemplating divorce is that they are usually preoccupied with what is going wrong in the marriage. They not only focus on the lows, but the low of the lows. Each partner can document the times and places where the marriage began to suffer from either internal or external stresses. The internal ones we often bring on ourselves. And the external ones frequently arise outside the marriage. We usually have little control over the latter.

The more a couple is preoccupied with what is wrong with the relationship, the lower they seem to sink. Indeed, many of us gauge our marriages by the low of the lows and constantly remind ourselves how bad things are or have been.

Perhaps we concentrate too much on these difficult times. Almost every marriage will experience less-than-desirable times because relatively few can continue a happily-ever-after, Paul-and-Patti-Perfect relationship. During the times we may be experiencing a few lows, we ought to think of and plan for some highs.

With the hectic pace of contemporary living, most couples will roller-coaster through life experiencing times of exuberance and other times of discouragement. Even during stressful times, most couples can and should recall some pleasant times they have shared together in the past. It is extremely important to remind ourselves and each other of these good experiences. What have been the highlights of marriage thus far? What were the contributing circumstances? Could we create these or similar experiences again?

If we plan and experience some good times along with the difficult ones, we will have something to cushion the lows when they do occur. And by so doing we immensely increase our capacity to survive in marriage. Since we have experienced good times together in the past, we have the same capacity to experience them again, if we both choose to do so.

Socrates once noted, "If all our misfortunes were laid in one common heap whence everyone must take an equal portion, most people would be content to take their own and depart." Perhaps the same is true of marriage.

Decisions about Divorce

One of the most sensitive decisions a couple will ever face is whether or not to terminate their marriage. At the present time, about 40 percent of couples in the United States eventually choose to do so. How many other couples seriously contemplate divorce is not presently known.

There are at least four categories of couples who contemplate divorce:

1. Those who divorce and later feel it was the correct decision.

2. Those who divorce and later feel it was the incorrect decision.

3. Those who remain married and later feel it was the correct decision.

4. Those who remain married and later feel it was the incorrect decision.

Whether or not a couple should stay married or divorce is a decision that only they can make, since they are the ones who will experience the consequences of the decision. Advice may be given, both solicited and unsolicited, but ultimately the couple must decide.

Those who are married and are seriously contemplating divorce may be interested in the research of Dr. Richard B. Stuart, who recently wrote an interesting book entitled *Helping Couples Change.* Dr. Stuart is a professor of Family and Community Medicine at the University of Utah.

In his book, Dr. Stuart notes, "The acid test of the wisdom of divorce can be found only in an assessment of its effects. While it has been shown that divorce and separation have devastating effects on most of those who move apart, many individuals thrive on the new freedom of separate living."[1]

According to Dr. Stuart, many couples in stressful marriages look only at the apparent advantages of divorce. These may include: (1) freedom from domestic routines; (2) an opportunity to rear children without the opposition of the other parent; (3) freedom from conflict with a troubled spouse; (4) an opportunity to control one's own resources and life space; and (5) opportunities to make personally fulfilling choices without constraint through the need to consider the wishes of another.

But Dr. Stuart warns that divorce is often not a blessing. He reviews many studies that indicate that the physical and mental health of divorced individuals is often less than the health of those whose marriages remain intact. Divorced individuals, he concludes, have higher mortality rates, higher suicide rates, higher rates of victimization through homicide, higher rates of fatal auto accidents, and increased sickness, particularly coronary diseases and cancer of the digestive organs. Divorced people also appear to be at risk for mental disorders. Dr. Stuart points out that the risk rate of the formerly married exceeds those of the married by as much as twenty-fold in certain categories.

Dr. Stuart also reports that few individuals benefit economically from divorce, particularly husbands. The U.S. Bureau of Census has shown that the average annual incomes of married men are significantly greater than those of men who are separated, divorced, widowed, or never married. So great is the economic disruption of divorce that one researcher observed that divorce is a stronger correlate of poverty than is race.

Before a couple decides to divorce, they should carefully examine the consequences on both sides of the ledger. Will the perceived advantages outweigh the potential disadvantages?

It may be found, Dr. Stuart concludes, that the many benefits of trying to improve the marriage may far outweigh the eventual stresses contingent on separation.

Crabgrass and Marriage

I once wrote a column in the *Deseret News* noting that most married couples become discouraged at times and that some want to terminate the relationship. Because of some of the unpleasant experiences in marriage, we may be tempted to seek divorce and start over, if possible, with someone else. And certainly in some instances divorce is justified. But there may be danger in uprooting something with potential good just to get rid of something that temporarily appears to be bad.

Susan and I learned this not long ago when we planted grass in our backyard. As it started to grow, so did the crabgrass. So many neighbors and friends had told us about the crabgrass in our new lawn that we soon began to believe the crabgrass would prevail. The neighborhood consensus was that the lawn could not survive. The crabgrass was so tall that the little blades of new lawn were barely visible.

One neighbor told us how to spray the yard with a certain

chemical that would kill everything. Then we could start over. Another neighbor offered us his Rototiller. We were discouraged, to say the least. It had taken us several months even to get this far with our new lawn. We had had to dig up rocks, bring in topsoil, level the soil, and fertilize and prepare the area for the lawn seed.

While trying to decide what to do, I stopped by a greenhouse one day with a few samples of the crabgrass. I described my plight to an elderly man who looked as though he knew something about plants and grass. "That's nothing but orchard grass," he said. "Just give your new lawn a little more water, fertilizer, and time. As the new lawn grows, it will soon crowd out the crabgrass." We followed his advice and now have a backyard of beautiful, thriving lawn. And the crabgrass is gone.

Marriage, too, has its discouraging moments. And sometimes we may want to give up the good in order to get rid of the bad. But the advice from the old man at the nursery still seems pertinent. Give your marriage a little more attention, make a little more effort, and the good experiences will eventually crowd out the bad ones. Focus your effort and attention on the lawn rather than on the crabgrass.

The importance of effort and focus, of believing and hoping, of bearing and enduring in marriage is emphasized in the poem "Listen World."

> *You can't leave love to luck.*
> *Love first came with leaping ecstasy.*
> *But when this passes . . . as it always may . . .*
> *Love, too, will go unless you make it stay.*
> *For there come times when hearts*
> *Are deaf and dumb, when nothing wakens,*
> *Nothing yearns or burns . . . These times must come;*
> *They are not accident, nor do they prove*
> *Your choice of love was wrong.*
> *They come with every lover,*
> *Every loving bond—mother or father,*
> *Sister, brother, mate. Always, at times,*

Love seems as cold as hate . . .
Cut off forever, by malignant fate.

But it's not so. Such chilling of the heart's
As much a part of life as thirst or hunger . . .
It's the natural ebb of our affection's flow.
Such times must come for all who love,
And when they come you must know why,
And how to meet them or your love will die.

You can't leave love to luck,
You must at times build love.
Though lacking all delight,
As blind men weave a pattern in the night,
Counting each gentle gesture,
Spacing word and smile, groping through darkness
Of both heart and head, as blind men fumble
With their unseen thread.
Until at last from out of the dull
Gray warp and woof of service, unto God and men,
There's the shine of that sweet wonder
Which you had thought had passed . . .
And, once again, you feel God's beautiful design.[2]

A Letter

I received a rather lengthy letter from a woman who described several difficult years of marriage. I read her letter often when I need motivation to continue writing about marriage. The woman mentioned some attempts, none of which worked, to improve the relationship. Divorce seemed more and more of a possibility as she and her husband began to drift apart.

She wrote:

> One day I was reading an article on marriage in the *Deseret News.* I usually don't like to read things like that because they always seem so idealistic and unattainable. But this article seemed to have some common sense and was down

to earth. The particular article was one in which you compared crabgrass to marriage. . . .

After reading your article . . . I cried and cried. I had cried before, but never do I remember feeling the way I did after reading what you wrote. I realized that deep inside I really did love my husband. And I was relieved to find a workable solution to a very difficult problem.

So I decided to try to "build love," as the poem "Listen World" suggested. I started writing notes of appreciation to my husband. They were just short notes telling him thanks for something or sharing with him a crazy poem. He didn't say or do anything the first day or for several days after that.

Then one night we got into an argument, and I thought, "Here we go again." Later that evening (we weren't talking) he came into the kitchen and put his arms around me. He gave me a big hug that broke the awful tension. It was the beginning of many more hugs, kisses, and talks that we needed.

We have a long way to go in our marriage, but I think maybe we can now make it. It will take a lot of work because learning how to love seems to be incredibly difficult. But it now looks feasible thanks to a poem and newspaper article on crabgrass and marriage.

A Marital Guide

In conclusion, may I share with you some thoughts of Dr. Virginia Satir about marriage. They ought to be read often by husbands and wives.

> I want to love you . . . without clutching.
> I want to appreciate you . . . without judging.
> I want to invite you . . . without demanding.
> I want to ask you . . . without pleading.
> I want to leave you . . . without guilt feelings.
> I want to join you . . . without invading.
> I want to criticize you . . . without blaming.
> I want to help you . . . without insulting.
> If I can have the same from you, we can meet and truly enrich each other.[3]

It is my hope that this book in some small way will help married couples want to do these things. And I give my sincere encouragement to husbands and wives to strive to do so. Marriage truly can become an exultant ecstasy if we want it to be and are willing to work for it. May we so commit ourselves, and then do it!

APPENDIX A

UNDERSTANDING YOUR EXPECTATIONS

While no wife can do all of the things below equally well at the same time, she can and perhaps should do some.

As a husband, review these items and then rank in order the ten characteristics most important to you in your marriage. For instance, if number nine is the most important, rank it first. If number four is second most important, rank it second. Continue until you have indicated the *ten* characteristics you would presently value most in a loving wife.

Rank Order

_____ 1. She is willing to give up certain things for the sake of our marital relationship.

_____ 2. She keeps our home reasonably clean and free from excessive clutter.

_____ 3. She prepares nutritious meals and serves them in a pleasant atmosphere and surroundings.

_____ 4. She helps me attain my spiritual needs.

_____ 5. She communicates effectively both by listening and speaking.

_____ 6. She helps me attain sexual satisfaction in our relationship.

_____ 7. She is aware that her appearance and physical fitness affect how I feel toward her.

_____ 8. She supports me in my endeavors both at home and at work.

_____ 9. She is patient with me and does not nag or complain excessively.

_____ 10. She expresses her love both by word and action.

_____ 11. She has high self-esteem.

_____ 12. She strives for intellectual growth and keeps herself informed about current events.

_____ 13. She has a sense of humor.

_____ 14. She is independent in addition to growing with me.

_____ 15. She gives our children adequate emotional and physical care.

_____ 16. She does not worry excessively.

_____ 17. She makes an effort to get along with my parents.

_____ 18. She often expresses herself by sharing her thoughts and feelings with me.

_____ 19. She allows time for me to be alone, when necessary.

_____ 20. She has me high in her priorities, even before the children.

After you have completed this exercise, you may want to share your results with your wife. You may also want to compare your results with the "Profile of a Loving Wife" (Appendix B).

APPENDIX B

PROFILE OF A LOVING WIFE

These are the ten most important items (in rank order) indicated by husbands in the *Deseret News* and marriage seminar surveys:

1. She expresses her love both by word and action.
2. She helps me attain my spiritual needs.
3. She supports me in my endeavors both at home and at work.
4. She gives our children adequate emotional and physical care.
5. She helps me attain sexual satisfaction in our relationship.
6. She communicates effectively both by listening and speaking.
7. She keeps our home reasonably clean and free from excessive clutter.
8. She is patient with me and does not nag or complain excessively.
9. She has high self-esteem.
10. She is aware that her appearance and physical fitness affect how I feel toward her.

NOTES

Preface

[1]Spencer W. Kimball, *Marriage and Divorce,* Salt Lake City: Deseret Book Company, 1976, p. 16.

[2]Hugh B. Brown, *You and Your Marriage,* Salt Lake City: Bookcraft, 1960, p. 107.

Chapter 1: Love

[1]Erich Fromm, *The Art of Loving,* New York: Bantam Books, 1956, preface.

[2]William J. Lederer and Don D. Jackson, *The Mirages of Marriage,* New York: W. W. Norton & Company, 1968, p. 40.

[3]David H. Olson, "Marriage of the Future: Revolutionary or Evolutionary Change?" *The Family Coordinator,* vol. 12, 1972, pp. 385-86.

[4]William George Jordan, "Little Problems of Married Life," *Improvement Era,* July 1911, p. 788.

[5]Edward Bader and Carole Sinclair, "The Critical First Year of Marriage," paper presented at the annual meeting of the National Council on Family Relations, October 16, 1981, Milwaukee, Wisconsin.

[6]Quoted by Larry Hof and William R. Miller in *Marriage Enrichment, Philosophy, Process and Program,* Bowie, Maryland: Robert J. Brady Co., 1981, pp. 105-6.

[7]Roland S. Larson and Doris E. Larson, *I Need to Have You Know Me,* Minneapolis: Winston Press, 1979, pp. 11-12.

[8]John F. Cuber and Peggy B. Harroff, *Sex and the Significant Americans,* Baltimore: PenguinBooks, 1965, pp. 43-65.

[9]Dick McDonald and Paula McDonald, *Loving Free,* New York: Ballantine Books, 1976, pp. 267-68.

[10]Anne Morrow Lindbergh, *War Within and Without,* New York: Harcourt, Brace, Jovanovich, 1980, p. 254.

Chapter 2: Spirituality

[1]Joseph Smith, *Teachings of the Prophet Joseph Smith,* selected by Joseph Fielding Smith, Salt Lake City: Deseret Book, 1938, pp. 255-56.
[2]Stephen L Richards, *Conference Report,* April 1920, p. 96.
[3]David O. MacKay, *Conference Report,* April 1920, p. 116.
[4]Harold B. Lee, *Ensign,* February 1974, p. 77.
[5]Spencer W. Kimball, *Church News,* January 5, 1974, p. 14.
[6]David O. McKay, *Conference Report,* April 1920, p. 116.
[7]*Journal of Discourses* 13:175.
[8]Lloyd Saxton, *The Individual, Marriage, and the Family,* Belmont, California: Wadsworth Publishing Company, 1968, p. 258.
[9]Edward J. Rydman, in *Handbook of Marriage Counseling,* Ben N. Ard, Jr., and Constance Ard, eds., Palo Alto: Science and Behavior Books, Inc., 1969, p. vii.
[10]Joseph F. Smith, *Gospel Doctrine,* 5th ed., Salt Lake City: Deseret Book Company, 1939, pp. 286-87.
[11]Edward Kimball, *Teachings of Spencer W. Kimball,* Salt Lake City: Bookcraft, 1982, p. 316.
[12]Smith, *Gospel Doctrine,* p. 287.
[13]Ibid., pp. 287-88.
[14]Rydman, *Handbook,* p. vii.
[15]Smith, *Gospel Doctrine,* pp. 287-88.
[16]Hoff and Miller, *Marriage Enrichment,* p. 155.
[17]Ibid., pp. 156-57. (Adapted.)

Chapter 3: Support

[1]E. E. LeMasters, *Parents in Modern America,* Homewood, Illinois: Dorsey Press, 1970, pp. 138-56.
[2]Ibid., p. 149.
[3]Ibid., p. 152.
[4]Joyce Brothers, *What Every Woman Should Know about Men,* New York: Simon and Schuster, 1981, p. 55.
[5]Richard K. Kerckhoff, "Marriage and Middle Age," *Family Coordinator,* January 1976, pp. 5-10.

Chapter 4: Motherhood

[1]James Dobson, *Dare to Discipline,* Wheaton, Illinois: Tyndale House Publishers, 1970, p. 23.
[2]Ibid., pp. 20-21.
[3]Ibid., pp. 23-50.
[4]*Journal of Discourses* 10:360-61.
[5]Dobson, *Dare to Discipline,* pp. 218-24.
[6]Evelyn Millis Duvall, *Family Development,* New York: J. B. Lippincott Company, 1971, p. 121.
[7]*Journal of Discourses* 13:61.
[8]*Journal of Discourses* 12:374-75.
[9]Barbara B. Smith, "Her Children Arise Up, and Call Her Blessed," *Ensign,* May 1982, pp. 79-81.

Chapter 5: Sexuality

[1]Mike Grace and Joyce Grace, *A Joyful Meeting: Sexuality in Marriage,* Saint Paul: International Marriage Encounter, 1980, pp. 65-78.

[2]Ibid., p. 74

[3]Ibid., p. 73.

[4]Ibid., pp. 74-75.

[5]Ibid., p. 76.

[6]Ibid., p. 77.

[7]Billy Graham, "What the Bible Says about Sex," *Reader's Digest,* May 1970, p. 118.

[8]The concept of sexual stewardships has been previously discussed and perhaps introduced by Carlfred B. Broderick. For a discussion on stewardships in marriage see his article "Midlife Report," *Ensign,* July 1979, pp. 28-30, and his interview on "A Gospel Centered Therapy," *Dialogue,* summer 1980, vol. 13, no. 2, pp. 59-75.

[9]D.Corydon Hammond and Robert F. Stahmann, "Sex Therapy with LDS Couples," *Journal of Association of Mormon Counselors and Psychotherapists,* January 1982, vol. 8, no. 1, pp. 13-16.

[10]Val D. MacMurray, "Sexual and Emotional Intimacy: A Need to Emphasize Principles," *Journal of Association of Mormon Counselors and Psychotherapists,* January 1982, vol. 8, no. 1, pp. 18-19.

Chapter 6: Communication

[1]David and Vera Mace, *How to Have a Happy Marriage,* Nashville: Abingdon, 1977, pp. 71-72.

[2]Richard B. Stuart, *Helping Couples Change,* New York: The Gilford Press, 1980, p. 222.

[3]Ibid., p. 224.

[4]Albert Ellis and Robert Harper, *A Guide to Successful Marriage,* Hollywood, California: Wilshire, 1972, pp. 190-208.

[5]Ibid., p. 204.

[6]Ibid., p. 205.

[7]Virginia Satir, *Peoplemaking,* Palo Alto: Science and Behavior Books, Inc., 1972, p. 77.

[8]*Marriage Encounter,* August 1982, vol. 11, no. 8, p. 24.

[9]Carlfred B. Broderick, *Couples: How to Confront Problems and Maintain Loving Relationships,* New York: Simon and Schuster, 1979, p. 84.

[10]Quoted in Richard Wilke, *Tell Me Again, I'm Listening,* Nashville: Abingdon, 1973, p. 135.

Chapter 7: Self-Esteem

[1]*Family Weekly,* August 1, 1982, p. 18.

[2]*Improvement Era,* July 1968, p. 63.

[3]Ellis and Harper, *A Guide to Successful Marriage,* p. 79.

[4]Lloyd Saxton, *The Individual, Marriage, and the Family,* Belmont, California: Wadsworth Publishing Company, 1980, p. 363.

[5]Ibid.

[6]Satir, *Peoplemaking,* pp. 27-29.

[7]Ibid.

[8]Robert H. Schuller, *Possibility Thinking,* series of audiotapes produced by Nightingale Conant Corp., 3730 West, Devon Avenue, Chicago, Illinois, 60656. Cassette tape number 7, "Self-Esteem."

[9]Carlfred Broderick, *Marriage and the Family,* New Jersey: Prentice-Hall, 1979, p. 80.

[10]*Ensign,* January 1974, pp. 2-6.

[11]*Teachings of the Prophet Joseph Smith,* p. 134.

[12]Zora Smith Jarvis, comp., *George A. Smith Family,* Provo, Utah: Brigham Young University Press, 1962, p. 54.

[13]*Foundations for Temple Marriage,* Salt Lake City: The Church of Jesus Christ of Latter-day Saints, 1979, p. 2.

[14]Truman Madsen, *The Highest in Us,* Salt Lake City: Bookcraft, 1978, p. 12.

Chapter 8: Homemaker

[1]Alvin Toffler, *Future Shock,* New York: Bantam Books, 1971, p. 238.

[2]Christopher Lasch, *Haven in a Heartless World: The Family Besieged,* New York: Basic Books, p. xiii.

[3]James B. Simpson, ed., *Contemporary Quotations,* New York: Cromwell Co., 1964, p. 238.

[4]Salt Lake *Tribune,* January 31, 1982, p. 10.

[5]Barbara B. Smith, "A Safe Place for Marriage and Families," *Ensign,* November 1981, p. 84.

[6]Deniece Schofield, *Confessions of an Organized Housewife,* Bountiful, Utah: The Idea Center, 1981, pp. 141-42.

[7]Richard L. Evans, "Clean—What a Wonderful Word," *Improvement Era,* January 1970, p. 32.

[8]David C. Willis and Harold Fondren, "Burnout in the Home," *Journal of the Association of Mormon Counselors and Psychotherapists,* April 1982, vol. 8, no. 2, pp. 19-20.

[9]Ibid.

[10]Ibid.

[11]Caroline Bird, *The Two-Paycheck Marriage,* New York: Rawson, Wade Publishers, 1979, p. 85.

[12]Federal income taxes represent the increase in the family's tax liability after the $10,000 has been added to the husband's $20,000 (using 1982 tax rates and assuming itemized deductions of $4,000 in excess of the zero bracket amount).

[13]This assumes that the wife buys additional clothing and accessories yearly to wear to work beyond what she would purchase if she stayed home.

[14]This includes the trend for an employed wife to receive a shampoo ($10) three times a month, a cut and style ($20) once a month, and a permanent ($50) four times a year. The wife who is not employed outside the home is assumed to have one shampoo a month, a cut and style four times a year, and a permanent only once a year.

[15]Food expenditures could increase as much as $50 a month because the employed wife buys lunch, purchases more convenience foods, eats out more often with the family, and greatly reduces the home production of food. Many families have found that their food bills have increased even more than $50 a month.

[16]This assumes the wife travels ten miles a day to and from work at twenty cents a mile (national average for 1982 is closer to forty cents a mile) and works fifty weeks a year.

[17]Fringe benefits may make returning to work somewhat more financially attractive, but would not materially change this analysis.

[18]The family may experience increased costs in other areas when the wife no longer works full-time at home. Explicit costs incurred would cover professional house cleaning, laundering, and yard work. Implicit costs focus on reduced efficiency in the maintenance of the home after the wife is employed. The total explicit and implicit costs actually may exceed in some cases the financial contribution by the wife to the family income.

Chapter 9: Attractiveness

[1]Brothers, *What Every Woman Should Know about Men,* pp. 221-22.

[2]Ibid.

[3]Elaine Walster and G. William Walster, *A New Look at Love,* Reading, Massachusetts: Addison-Wesley Publishing Company, 1978, p. 149.

[4]Saxton, *The Individual, Marriage, and the Family,* p. 249.

[5]Provo *Daily Herald,* February 8, 1982.

[6]Alexandra Penney, *How to Make Love to a Man,* New York: Dell Publishing Co., 1981, p. 55.

[7]Ibid., pp. 54-56.

[8]David O. McKay, *Gospel Ideals,* Salt Lake City: Improvement Era, 1953, p. 450.

[9]Spencer W. Kimball, "Marriage is Honorable," *Speeches of the Year,* 1973, Provo, Utah: Brigham Young University Press, 1974, pp. 261-62.

[10]Sterling W. Sill, "To Die Well," *Ensign,* November 1976, p. 48.

[11]*Deseret News,* July 1, 1982.

[12]*Health and Wealth,* Salt Lake City: Deseret Mutual Benefit Association, vol. 1, no. 8, spring 1982, p. 4.

[13]Tim and Beverly LaHaye, *The Act of Marriage: A Christian Guide to Sexual Love,* New York: Bantam Books, 1978, pp. 129-30.

[14]*Family Weekly,* July 25, 1982, p. 13.

[15]Jean Mayer, *Overweight: Causes, Cost, and Control,* Englewood Cliffs: Prentice-Hall, 1968, p. 203.

[16]*Journal of Discourses* 13:154.

[17]*Journal of Discourses* 2:269-70.

[18]Sterling G. Ellsworth and Richard G. Ellsworth, *Getting to Know the Real You,* Salt Lake City: Deseret Book Company, 1980, pp. 86-88.

[19]Ibid., pp. 10-11.

Final Comments

[1]Richard B. Stuart, *Helping Couples Change,* New York: The Guilford Press, 1980, p. 8.

[2]Quoted in Louis H. Evans, *Your Marriage, Duel or Duet?* Westward, New Jersey: F. H. Revell Co., 1962, p. 72.

[3]Quoted in Dick and Paula McDonald, *Loving Free,* New York: Ballantine Books, 1976, preface.

INDEX